D1784180

TESTIFY

TESTIFY

AUGUST LOVE

COPYRIGHT © 2019 BY AUGUST LOVE.

LIBRARY OF CONGRESS CONTROL NUMBER:		2019911400
ISBN:	HARDCOVER	978-1-7960-5040-0
	SOFTCOVER	978-1-7960-5039-4
	EBOOK	978-1-7960-5038-7

All rights reserved. No part of this book may be reproduced or transmitted in any form or by any means, electronic or mechanical, including photocopying, recording, or by any information storage and retrieval system, without permission in writing from the copyright owner.

Scripture quotations marked KJV are from the Holy Bible, King James Version (Authorized Version). First published in 1611. Quoted from the KJV Classic Reference Bible, Copyright © 1983 by The Zondervan Corporation.

Scripture taken from The Holy Bible, English Standard Version® (ESV®), copyright © 2001 by Crossway, a publishing ministry of Good News Publishers. Used by permission. All rights reserved.

Scripture quotations marked AMP are from The Amplified Bible, Old Testament copyright © 1965, 1987 by the Zondervan Corporation. The Amplified Bible, New Testament copyright © 1954, 1958, 1987 by The Lockman Foundation. Used by permission. All rights reserved.

The Holy Bible, Berean Study Bible, BSB
Copyright ©2016, 2018 by Bible Hub
Used by Permission. All Rights Reserved Worldwide.

Scripture taken from the New King James Version®. Copyright © 1982 by Thomas Nelson. Used by permission. All rights reserved.

Holy Bible, New International Version®, NIV® Copyright ©1973, 1978, 1984, 2011 by Biblica, Inc.® Used by permission. All rights reserved worldwide.

Holy Bible, New Living Translation, copyright © 1996, 2004, 2015 by Tyndale House Foundation. Used by permission of Tyndale House Publishers, Inc., Carol Stream, Illinois 60188. All rights reserved.

American Standard Version (ASV)
Public Domain

The Message (MSG)
Copyright © 1993, 2002, 2018 by Eugene H. Peterson

Any people depicted in stock imagery provided by Getty Images are models, and such images are being used for illustrative purposes only.
Certain stock imagery © Getty Images.

Print information available on the last page.

Rev. date: 08/22/2019

To order additional copies of this book, contact:
Xlibris
1-888-795-4274
www.Xlibris.com
Orders@Xlibris.com
800131

CONTENTS

PRAYER

Father, in the name of Jesus, I want to first thank you for being Lord of my life. For without you I can do nothing, and without you I am nothing. You are my lifeline. You're the reason I'm here today. I am beyond grateful to know that you would save someone like me, not worthy of your grace or mercy, but so thankful that you look beyond my faults and saw my needs.

Thank you for giving me the mind to seek your face for instruction, understanding, and wisdom. Thank you for allowing me to be transparent in the writing of this book, and for giving me the strength to look within myself, knowing that you've placed everything in me that I need to accomplish it!

You've given me the strength to look beyond my fears, pain, and disappointments, and within that you remind me that "I can do all things through Christ" because you will strengthen me.

My prayer, God, is that this book will be a blessing and provider strength to everyone who reads it, and encouragement to everyone who needs it. I ask that you rebuke every spirit of fear and every spiritual stronghold over the minds of your people, and set them free by the power that is within you.

Thank you for the spirit of love and forgiveness. You forgave us, so that we can forgive others! This is my humble prayer, in Jesus's name. Amen!

THANK YOU

I want to take this opportunity to say "thank you" to my family (Mother), friends, church family, and prayer partners for believing in and praying for me. I solicit your prayers, and you followed through. I called and you answered. Sometimes you listened and sometimes you would give advice, but whatever your role, I just want to say I am beyond grateful!

To my wonderful leaders, **Bishop Gary L. Hall**, and **First Lady Mary L. Hall**, thank you for building upon the foundation that was laid. Jeremiah 3:15 (KJV) states, "And I will give you pastors according to mine heart, which shall feed you with knowledge and understanding."

To the fragrance of the house, First Lady Hall, I love you to life. I have learned so much from you over the years. You are a virtuous woman indeed. Continue to allow God to use you!

To the best leader on this side of heaven, Bishop Hall, someone once said to me, "Your pastor is a gold-digger." At first, I thought, "What?" but then she went on to explain, "He is such an awesome teacher; he tries his best to get every nugget out of God's word!" So, I'll say to you, Keep digging, sir, and continue to give God your permission and your participation.

INTRODUCTION

Thank you for taking this journey down memory lane with me. I pray that my testimony will be a blessing to you or someone you know who has dealt with or dealing with some of the things I've been through. I know it might not be easy to talk about, but I pray that this book will help guild you in the right direction.

Sometimes we question why God allows what he allows to happen in our lives, and wonder if there's an expiration date to our trouble, screaming, "Lord, when will it end?" But Ecclesiastes 3:1 says, "To everything there is a season, and a time to every purpose under the heaven," Ecclesiastes 3:1 KJV, and according to Romans 8:28, it states, "And we know that all things work together for good to them that love God, to them who are the called according to his purpose"! So yes, I understand it gets hard, but be encouraged and know that God is still in control, and his plan is to bring us to an expected end according to Jeremiah 29:11, "For I know the thoughts that I think toward you, saith the Lord, thoughts of peace, and not of evil, to give you an expected end." Jeremiah 29:11 KJV

As I put pen to paper, I sat and wonder, why would God choose me of all people to write this book? This question ran through my mind for the longest. "Why me of all people?" I'm not the smartest or the most articulate. I'm not a writer, and I consider myself to be the least qualified. Then the answer hit me in the form of a question. "So how is God going to get the glory if you're not willing to tell your story?" But in my mind, I honestly felt like I didn't have a story to tell! Therefore, I had to take a step back and *pray*! Now, if you ever heard me pray, you most likely heard me say these words, "Lord, come get your glory" (I believe it was a setup). Okay, let me drop this in here and tell you why I believe it was a setup! I never started praying, "Lord, come get your glory" until my church choir released a CD live at the Ritz and my pastor preached a seven-minute message and he titled that message "Lord, come get your glory," and for whatever the reason, I couldn't shake it. And every time I opened my mouth to pray those words would fly out, and from that day until now those five words have always been a part of my prayer! Little did I know God was planning a seed. God is strategic in how he plans out our lives. We're thinking one way, but he has something totally different in mind! As far as the north is from the south, and the east from the west, God is always a thousand steps ahead of us.

(I know my thoughts toward you, says the Lord.)

People often say, "Sometimes you have to get out of your comfort zone in order for God to get the glory out of your life." Well, can I just say, there is no comfort in this zone . . . None whatsoever!

Everyone has a story, some more beautiful than others, and some more traumatic, but at the end of the day, it's still your story!

This book is not about me becoming an author, but rather the Author coming to me and instructing me on how to write my story. Where it goes from there is up to him.

CHAPTER 1

IN THE BEGINNING

For thou hast possessed my reins: thou has covered me in my mother's womb. I will praise thee; for I am fearfully and wonderfully made: marvelous are thy works; and that my soul knoweth right well (Ps. 139:13–14, KJV).

HOW IT CAME ABOUT

It's funny how I sit and reflect on how my friend, Regina, and I used to sit around the house and talk about our upbringing. We would talk about all the crazy things we've experienced on this road called life. She would always say, "You need to write a book on your life story," and we would just laugh! To me that was the funniest thing because I had some funny stories, but I was thinking, who would want to read about my life! As the saying goes, it was like water of a ducks back because I knew she was joking, and I really didn't think I had anything that important to say!

Years later I was in a church service, and as the pastor was praying, she called for me, and she began to prophesy to me. As she hit my hand, she said to me, "You have a book in you that you need to write!" My first thought was, "Really, lady . . . yeah, right!" Um no, but okay, if you say so! So I went home and forgot all about it. Then I called to remembrance a dream I had, thinking maybe I do, but about what? I didn't want to assume, so I left it alone again and went on with my life.

A year or so later, I experienced some turbulence in my life and a few hurricanes, and I found myself in the wilderness that caused me to relocate mentally, to say the least! Everything that I thought could go wrong did! In addition, everything

I didn't think of did also. I thought, God, what is really going on! Well, here I am writing this book, so I guess I'll "testify"!

HISTORY

I was born in the beautiful island of Nassau, Bahamas. We moved to Miami when I was nine years old. I am one of twelve children; yes, I come from a big family, as you can see. We did not all grow up in the same household at the same time, but we were all close. I am the sixth child of my mother's and the firstborn of my father!

GROWING UP

From what I can remember, I had a happy childhood growing up (pre-teen). My mom and dad were pretty good parents. They made sure we had food to eat, clothes on our backs, and a roof over our heads. That's what was important to them. We didn't have a lot, but we didn't know it at the time, nor did we complain about what we didn't have.

We didn't get to play outside much, and unlike today, back then it was a big deal. Did we get the latest toys for Christmas? No, we got what they could afford and were thankful. Did you say, "What about birthday parties?" Nope! (Yeah, I know how sad you're thinking!) My first birthday party was given to me by my adopted godmother, Bernadette, and it was for my fourteenth birthday. She treated me like the daughter she never had. But don't get me wrong, our birthdays did not go unnoticed. My mom would always bake cakes for our birthdays, and she baked them from scratch! That was special because if it was your birthday, you got to lick the bowl, while your siblings got the spoons. Ah, fun times. We had each other. You didn't hear it a lot, but love was implied.

Then the word of the Lord came unto me, saying, Before I formed thee in the belly I knew thee; and before thou camest forth out of the womb I sanctified thee, and I ordained thee a prophet unto the nations (Jer. 1:4). KJV

CHAPTER 2

DOWN MEMORY LANE

My stress started in junior high school! I had to deal with a lot of name-calling and dirty looks. Do you know how it feels to be called ugly or to be picked on? Being bullied as a teen was not cool. I hated school! It was like the worst place in the world to be! It was like I got my first look into the realization that we were poor, and it seemed like everyone else looked better, dressed better, and ate better—they did everything better! That didn't bother me as much in the beginning; however, I did take notice. The children were mean, but the girls were worst! Someone always wanted to fight, but one thing about it: I never backed down from a fight! Scared or not! That was a no-no in my family. We were taught to defend ourselves! Well, it was my uncle, who will remain nameless, who stressed the importance of self-defense.

I couldn't tell you how many fights I got into because someone didn't like me or what I was wearing, or according to them I was this little skinny black ugly girl they thought they could push around; therefore that was a reason for them to want to fight me.

Nevertheless, the bullying left a scare that took years to heal. I was always smiling but secretly hating my life. As I was growing up, I would look in the mirror and hated what I saw looking back at me. (Thinking, that's only because someone said I was ugly or unattractive.) I was looking at myself the way others perceived me. I never saw who I was because all I see was what they saw. Even when I was called pretty, I would still feel ugly and think to myself, yeah, right! I know they're just saying that to make me feel good, but I never believed them. The one person, however, that I can say made it stick for a second for whatever the reason was my cousin, Maude. She would always say, "August, you are so pretty," and for some reason it rang in my ear! Her voice always seemed so sincere.

When I was growing up, my parents didn't affirm or validate us as children. I don't think they felt they had to! Well, for me I don't recall, so when I was being called names, there was no counterbalance. I had nothing to weigh it against! So, the ugly outweighed the pretty and that's what I considered myself to be most of my life! It was to the point when a guy would try and talk to me, I would not make eye contact because of feeling the fear of rejection. If a guy found me attractive, in my mind he wanted or was up to something!

To me, all my sisters are beautiful! I would look at them and think, Wow, they are so pretty, and everyone noticed it too! I never heard anyone call my sisters ugly! Therefore, I asked God why I had to be the ugly one in the family, almost like the black sheep! It was one of the most painful times in my life, even more so because I kept it all inside.

No one knew what or how I was feeling. I know it should not have mattered what people thought of me, but back then it did. I never, however, let it stop me from walking with my head up high. You know, as the old saying goes, "Never let them see you sweat." So I had to walk with a smile on my face, but on the inside, I was sometimes hating the face I saw in the mirror.

When I talked about how I felt or looked, people were quick to quote the scripture, "You're fearfully and wonderfully made," but with my "have to analyze everything" mind, I was looking for "pretty." Yeah, I was *wonderfully* made in creation, but why was I made ugly, was my question! Look, if you've never had to fight with your mirror, or been picked on because of the way you look, or called out of your name, you will never understand the mind of someone who has!

Some things, if not dealt with, will grow up with you, alongside you, reminding you of your past, trying to prevent you from focusing on your future and the plan God has for you. So, don't say to someone, "It doesn't matter" or that "It happened to you as a child so let it go!" Sorry to disappoint you, but it is not that easy. This is deeper than you think. This is spiritual bondage and the struggle is real! Some things take time to let go of, but it must be addressed. My bishop used to say a long time ago, "If you don't face it, God can't fix it"! So, I had to start facing some things, and there are some things we all must face.

I remember one year, still in junior high, I was in the chorus, and we had to sing in a Christmas musical. We had to wear red and white as part of our uniform. I didn't have the colors, so my mom decided she was going to make my dress! She had this lime green material with white polka dots on it! (Yeah, I know . . . I can still see it.) Anyway, I tried stressing the importance of the colors to her because it was a "Christmas event," but personally, I think the sewing machine started singing in her head because she didn't listen to a word that came out of my mouth.

I'm not going to tell you I didn't want to participate anymore, and playing sick was out of the question! When I tell you, I looked like a giant glow in the dark key lime pie standing up there in the mist of all that red and white, I mean it! I promise you I have memory block from some parts of that night! That might be a good thing! This only added to the looks and name-calling bandwagon! Looking back, I felt like they could have taken a picture and used it as part of a child's homework lesson: "Which one of these colors does *not* belong?"

Parents, it's important that you validate your children, not their peers or classmates, not even their other siblings! Yes, they play a role, but it should start with you! My bishop said something that stuck with me years ago. He said, "You've never seen your face with your own eyes." Hmm, interesting, I thought! It's only through the reflection of a mirror that shows you your face. Therefore, you know how you look based on a mirror and/or the opinions of other people! Wow! So, I'll dare to ask, How do you see yourself now? I need you to pick up a mirror . . .

MIRROR* MIRROR *MIRROR
HOW DO YOU SEE YOURSELF NOW?

How do you feel when you look at the person in this mirror? Take another look! No, seriously, I want you to get a mirror and look at yourself! As a woman, are you afraid to leave the house without makeup on? If so, why? Too many dark spots or pimples? Is your forehead or nose too big? Are your lips too thin? Or maybe it's that big birthmark or mole on your face that causes you to feel a certain way? Maybe your chin is too wide or long, or your eyes are too big! Are you covering your ears with your hair, or do you feel like someone's always watching you?!

Do you know that there are some women who don't leave the house without makeup on? Funny, because most of them are the main ones to call other women ugly. Go figure! A lady once told me that her husband *never* saw her without makeup; she said she would wait for him to go to sleep before she took it off, or she would wake up before him to put it back on! I thought, How sad! (Thinking, I'm sure he wakes up through the middle of the night, but okay, tell your story.) You don't even love yourself enough to appreciate your own God-given beauty!

Don't get me wrong, I wear makeup from time to time too! But makeup should enhance you, not transform you!

Tell your daughters that they are beautiful, that they are cute or pretty no matter what anyone else says or thinks about them. Teach them how to love themselves. Remind them that God made them special and unique from everyone else. They're an original masterpiece and there's no one else like them. Encourage them every day to be all that God is calling them to be.

Fathers, date your daughters. Show them how a man is supposed to treat them so when Johnny-come-lately comes along, they won't fall for the games. Teach them the importance of keeping their virginity for marriage. Let them know that not every man has to test-drive before they make a down payment, and no, a lobster dinner does not equal sex. Let them know that their bodies are precious jewels and it is worth saving for their husband. (Not that once-upon-a-time, birds-and-bees conversation we used to have!) Tell them the truth or JR will tell them a lie! Trust me!

Remind them of how much you love them and that they mean the world to you. And tell your sons likewise, that they are handsome young men and that God created them to be leaders, mighty men of valor! And one day your hope for them is to marry a beautiful woman and raise children of their own. It's imperative that you speak *life* into your children. (I know this isn't something new you're hearing.) You have to give them the information; what they do with it is up to them, but you still have to give it to them. There are so many places for them to learn in life other than home. Their school, their peers, the Internet, or just being out in the world, but the greatest impact should come from you!

"Train up a child in the way he (she) should go, and when he is old, he will not depart from it" (Prov. 22:6, KJV).

By the way, if you're not active in your children's lives, please get active. Please don't be an absentee parent! Your children need both parents active in their lives even if you don't live in the same home.

Were you a bully? _____ If your answer was yes, I ask that you pray (if not already) and ask God to forgive you for the pain you have caused in someone's life. This spirit is strong and is causing a lot of young people (even adults) to lose their lives. Only God knows how many have committed suicide because of it, or are still dealing with the pain or trauma *you* caused. No, they might not have looked like you or dressed like you, but they are God's creation and should have been treated and respected as such. This is not something you should be proud of or want on your conscience. God forgives you, and so do we. Trust me when I tell you, this is not something you want to reap!

Were you bullied? _____ If you answered yes to this question, I asked that you pray and ask God to heal your heavy heart, remove the pain, and forgive those that caused it! Tell yourself that you are strong and courageous, and that you can do "all things through Christ"! Trust me; he will give you the strength to do it! Forgiving them isn't just for them, it's also for you. Forgiving them lets you out of the cage you built for them.

Did you stand by and watched someone get bullied? _____ If your answer was also yes to this question, then I ask that you *repent* for standing by and doing nothing! Understanding, you could have been a voice of reasoning but for whatever the reason, perhaps fair, you did nothing, not ever report it!

If your answer was *no* to all the above, I still want you to pray for "all of the above" according to Romans 15:1. *"We then that are strong ought to bear the infirmities of the weak and not to please ourselves." KJV*

LET'S PRAY

Father, in the name of Jesus, I ask that you forgive us of our sins.

We pray concerning the sins that were committed and the sins that were omitted. Father, I pray for every person that was bullied and wore the scare of it for years. I pray that you would free them from this spiritual stronghold and free them from being trapped in the shadow of their past. For whom the Son sets free is free indeed. Your word declares that "you did not give us the spirit of fear, but of love, peace, and a strong mind," so I pray that your people will be transformed by the renewing of their minds. Father, restore as only you know how. We rebuke and cast down every "imagination (memory) and the high thing that would try to exalt itself against you." We pray for peace for the bullies, restoration for the bullied, and wisdom to all mankind, in Jesus's name. Amen.

CHAPTER 3

RELOCATION

The first time I left home, I went to Job corps (in Mississippi). It was the scariest experience of my life because I did not know what to expect going in! The first order of business was orientation. In orientation you got familiar with the people that came in with you; they were your orientation brothers and sisters. You pretty much did everything together for the first few weeks. The rules and regulations were addressed and their expectations of us. Everything we need on campus! With this came medical and dental check-up, a banking account, and allowances every two weeks. Since we were in the middle of the country, we were not able to leave the campus, so they provided a bus to take us out on the weekend to go shopping for clothing, snacks, or toiletries. We were provided with three meals a day, and there was a canteen to purchase snacks if needed.

In addition to that, we had classes five days a week based on our major/study of choice, and we were given weekly chores. They pretty much paid for all our off-campus activities such as skating, movies, theme parks, to name a few.

Being there allowed me to blossom in my own way. I became active in sports. I played baseball, basketball, and volleyball, and made my way up to captain of the cheerleading team.

We played against other Job Corp centers in the South—Alabama, Georgia, and Tennessee, including Mississippi! Our men's basketball team was unstoppable. Overall, we had more wins than losses.

I had my share of short-term relationships. Hahaha. I was young but wise! I did not allow my feelings to override my decisions, and because of it, a few people started saying I was a dike because I wasn't giving it up. No, I was smart! I knew I was not going to be there forever, and when I left, I didn't want to leave pregnant or other! Peer pressure was never an issue for me, so I didn't follow the crowd! I had my own mind and did what I thought was necessary for me, and if I knew the truth was all that really mattered.

I pretty much follow the guidelines! I was even pointed as a junior Resident Assistant. My overall experience there was great!

After leaving for the Christmas holiday, I decide to stay in Miami with my family, and because of it I didn't finish the program. My only regret was not keeping in touch with some of my friends. Sarah M. and I would write each other throughout the years, but then we lost contact! Notice I said write. Yeah, there were no cell phones or Internet back then.

After much consideration, I decided to go back and finish, but instead of going back to Mississippi I came to Jacksonville! The two places were like night and day!

From day one, some of the women tried to give me a hard time, and before the end of the month, someone wanted to fight me, and yes, his name was Leon!

One morning my orientation sister and I were at breakfast, and as we stood leaving to dump our trays, some of the young ladies, also known as the "bad girls' crew," were sitting up in the stands. Nevertheless, as were leaving, we heard them say, "Introducing the grand finale"! I didn't know what it meant, so I carried on with my day. Then, later, she said, "I think they were talking about you!" I was in disbelief; moreover, I thought that was crazy! She came up with a plan to test the theory, so she said, "Okay, if they are there during lunch when it's time to leave, I'll leave first, then you come after me." So, during lunch, they were all sitting there again, so we did as planned!

After we finished eating, she took her tray to empty it first and nothing happened, and then I took my tray, and when I walked by, they said it again, "Introducing the grand finale." So I did what I knew to do: I went back and took a bow! It seemed every time they saw me that had something negative to say, and their favorite saying was "She thinks she's cute"! (Note: My tongue was very sharp so if you come for me, be prepared for a comeback!) I heard it so much that I would reply, "No, you think I'm cute, so thank you for thinking it for me"! Yet I was thinking, "Child, if you really knew me, you would know that is so far from the truth." Howbeit I've always walked with my head up regardless of where I was or how I felt. I guess you can say I was confident, but not conceited! Crazy part is when they were by themselves; their mouths were like mountains.

Fast forward, I ran into one of them years later in a church service at church during one of our church meetings. She came up to me with a smile on her face asking if I remember her. I was like, "How can I forget when you tried to make my life a living hell," but I didn't say that; however, I was short with my speech. Hey, we were in church and I wasn't where I am now! They say time heals all wounds, but I don't know. I guess it all depends on what it was. However, I would dare to add, facing the issues and dealing with them allows you healing.

I had a lot more freedom at Job corps (in Florida). We could come and go as we pleased as long as we were in before curfew, and a weekend pass was available if we wanted to leave for the weekend!

The downtown Jacksonville was one of our hangouts. That place was always thick, and we had our fake IDs for Fat Tuesdays if we needed it! Not to mention various clubs with fake IDs on one hand and drinks on the other! Oh, and you know where you can find me—yes, on the dance floor!

After the program ended, I stayed in Jacksonville with my friend, Krysta, for a few months until I got the call that one of my brothers, Anthony, was shot and killed. As a result, I had to move back home. Fortunately for me, I stayed in touch with her and after a year or two, I moved back to Jacksonville.

It was a few days before my twenty-third birthday. That bus ride was scary and lonely; I think I cried off and on all the way to West Palm Beach. I was starting to have second thoughts, thinking, "Ooh my goodness, what did I get myself into," but there was no turning back. I was on a one-way trip to the Ville. My friends and family thought I was crazy and kept saying, "Oh she'll be back," but there was something driving me. I couldn't put my finger on it, but I knew I had to leave.

My plan was to move to Jacksonville, move into the WNC, get a job, then get my own apartment. Well, I stayed at the house of my friend Krysta's mom for the weekend. By Monday I moved into the WNC as planned, and a few weeks later I was working at grocery store. Almost a year later I started dating this young man name Carl. Carl was in the navy and during that time he was going out to sea two to three times a month, preparing for his six-month deployment.

He knew I was looking for an apartment and at the time he wanted to move off base, so he suggested that we move in together. After much consideration, we did, along with my friend, Krysta.

THE CHURCH

One evening we went down to the downtown Jacksonville for a night out. (It was the place to be back in the nineties.) But unfortunately, I lost my wallet with my driver's license and I had to get another one. Now, where we lived was not far from the drivers' license office. Besides, we've been there before. But on this day, Carl took the long route and I didn't know any better at the time because we were new to the Westside. Okay, so let me paint this picture for you. We lived on Jammes Road between San Juan and London Blvd, and the drivers' license place was on London Blvd off I-95 between Stone Rd. and Old Nelson Rd. Now, instead of him driving up to Wilson and making that right, which would have taken him right to the DMV, he instead drove past Wilson up to 3rd St, drove down 3rd St to Stone Rd., took that right, and drove back down to Wilson, made a left, and drove down to the DMV.

"Now what does that have to do with the price of rice in China?" you ask. Well, I'll be glad to answer that question! Okay, so let's back up. Since I moved to Jacksonville, I've been looking for a church home, a covering, if you will. I've visited numerous churches, but none grab my attention. As we were driving down Stone Rd., I noticed this church sitting off to my left, and it looked as if it was calling me! (I know it sounds crazy.) But it was like the heavens opened over it and I couldn't take my eyes off it until it was out of sight. I became speechless, because I never experienced anything like that before! When I got home, all I could do was think about that church, but I didn't remember how to find it. This is crazy for me because I can go anywhere one time and remember because that's how much I paid attention to my surroundings. When Krysta got home from work, I shared with her my experience and how I wanted to find that church!

Krysta started working at the discount store on 3rd St of Stone, and when I took her to work, we would always go up to 3rd St and down to Stone, and that's the same way I went back home. I was taking her to work one day and she said, "Hey, I know a shortcut," so I was cool with it. She said to take a right on Wilson, and when we got to Stone Rd., she said to make a left. As we were driving, I looked to my right and there it was again. I screamed in excitement! "Krysta, look, there it is—that's the church I saw!" When I dropped her off, I drove back by just to look at it again. There was no one outside, but as I looked at it, I promise you, it felt like it was calling me. I didn't know what kind of church it was or what kind of people went there. I didn't even read the sign out front. All I knew was there was something about that church and I wanted to know what it was.

During this time my friend was out to sea, so it was just Krysta and me. I woke up Sunday morning excited about going to church. I didn't know what time church started; I just knew eleven o'clock was the norm for most churches! It was the last Sunday in February, and when I walked in the door, I saw a lot of people in African attire. I thought to myself, "Is this an African church?" Nevertheless, I went on in. The people were friendly and loved to hug. It seems like every time someone spoke to me, they hugged me! I made sure to sit at the back of the church. I sat on the left side, on the second to the last pew, so I can get a full view of what was going on.

During the announcement, it was made clear as to why everyone was in African attire. They were celebrating Black History Month. I thought, okay, that makes sense. The music started playing, the choir started singing, and the people were all into it, clapping, dancing, and praising their God. I didn't know any of the songs or anyone there, so I just sat back and watched! After the praise and worship, they introduced the pastor to come forward. When he stood up, I was in awe! I said to myself, "That's the pastor," and when they introduced his wife, I was like, "That's his wife"! They both looked so young. I was expecting some old gray-haired bearded man because I never saw a pastor so young before! I wasn't focused on their name; I just wanted to know who the pastor was, so I'll know who to dodge after services.

Even though I felt at peace in that service, I was still a little distracted because I was busy watching everything and everyone around me. One of the ladies on the same row started crying, and another sister came and took her by the hand and started running around the church. Another one broke down in tears, crying unto the Lord. In that moment I knew I had to get the straight face quick and made sure no tears were falling from my eyes because I wasn't running anywhere with no one!

Now, it wasn't until the end of the services that I became a little uneasy, so I had to brace myself to say *no*, but the "no" never came because the pastor didn't have an altar call. Say what now! What kind of church is this? I've never been to a church where there was no altar call. This was a first for me! My first thought was, "He's not trying to make anyone get saved!" I thought, This is a cool church! (But I didn't know it was a setup.) The following weekend I went back; the same thing! Awesome services, people hugging each other, choir singing, people praising, and at the end of the services no altar call! I thought to myself, Oh, I love this church. The following Sunday I went back again. This time I'm more attentive, and the message was awesome. I'm a little more relaxed. The benediction was given, and we were out! I said to myself, The next time I come, I'm joining this church.

Now I know someone might be thinking, why would he go almost a month without making an altar call for salvation! Yeah, I thought the same thing. But when God has a plan for your life, he will stop time in time, just to make time for you. God knew me better than I knew myself. "O Lord, you have searched me [thoroughly] and have known me. You know when I sit down and when I rise up [my entire life, everything I do]. You understand my thought from afar" (Ps. 139:1–2, AMP)." See, he knows what we're thinking before it even enters our mind.

Now the following Sunday I didn't make it because I was invited to go down to Daytona for spring break. Considering I never went, I thought, Why not? Looking back now, all I can say is, Lord, thank you for saving me!

March 27, 1994. This is the day I decided I was going to join the West Jacksonville COGIC, under the leadership of Elder Gary L. Hall Sr. I was so excited, I couldn't wait for them to open the doors of the church, but that was short-lived because at the end of the service, Elder Hall decided to do an altar call! Wait, *what*?

As I stood in the back of that church, there was a war going on inside me. I was fussing. I was angry because I did not want to "repent" of my sins. I wanted to continue to live the life I was living and continue to go to church like I did when I was home! The best of both worlds, as I see it. The enemy was reminding me of what I was giving up! He said, What about your man friend? You know he'll be coming home soon. What about the clubs? You won't be able to go partying anymore. What about your friends that come up from Miami? What are they going to say when they find out you got saved and can't party with them anymore! I felt myself getting even angrier, then I heard a voice say, "If you don't go now . . ." That was it, and nothing else came behind it. But I felt everything that voice meant in those five words! I knew now was the time! It was just something about that voice that penetrated my soul. I know if I didn't go then, I might not have gotten the opportunity again! Before I knew it, I pushed the person standing next to me to the side, and by the time my feet hit the middle aisle, I broke! I couldn't tell you how I made it to the altar. I just knew when I opened my eyes, I was standing there with tears running down my face!

Why did I call it a setup? Well, my biggest issue with churches was the "altar call"! If I didn't leave before the altar call, I would have a strong *no* prepared! When the pastor started quoting Revelation talking about "Jesus said the day that you hear my voice, harden not your heart," well, mine was hardened before I left home for church. As the saying goes, "God knew my heart." Yes, he really did. He knew if there was an altar call on that first day, I might not have made it back, but most importantly I believe he also knew that the enemy had a trap set for me,

13

but he loved me so much he didn't let his plan succeed! The devil fought for me; he really did! But I'm so glad he didn't win!

I left church on cloud nine that Sunday. I saw myself skipping through a field of flowers in my mind. However, a few days later my reality started to kick in because I had to decide what I was going to do with my significant other still out on the sea. Something happened prior to salvation that had me wanting to end the relationship, but I decided to wait until he got home to talk about it! Now, when he got home, all hell broke loose because I've committed my life to Christ and my body was no longer my own. I would like to tell you that he understood after I gave him my reasoning, but I can't! He had no understanding whatsoever, especially after being on deployment for six long months.

Long story short, I moved out! (Yeah, I know, maybe I'll talk about it later.) I moved into a one-bedroom apartment on Lenox Avenue. I had no furniture, just a mattress I got from my neighbor, and a television, but I was happy and content! My job was not too far up the street so I would walk to work. I was working at the Hotel on Lane Avenue doing housekeeping. The downside to this job was working on Sundays. I was not able to make it to church like I used to. And because I wasn't there, the enemy started talking to me, telling me I was no longer saved or a Christian because I was no longer going to church, and because I was working every Sunday, I started believing the voice. But that was the trick the enemy played on me. Nevertheless, when my friends would visit from Miami, I found myself back in the clubs. The crazy part is, if I wasn't on the dance floor, I was probably talking to someone about Jesus! It was the craziest thing!

For the record, salvation is not about being in church. It's about having a relationship with God. "If you confess with your mouth the Lord Jesus and believe in your heart that God raised him from the dead you shall be saved," according to Romans 10:9. Keep in mind, you don't have to be in church to get saved (that can happen anywhere . . . even now if you're not!), but you need to go especially if you're able to! "Forsake not the assembly," according to Hebrews 10:25, but just because you're not there doesn't mean you're no longer saved! You can still read your word and pray until God opens that door for you to go!

I remember one night we were going out to club to the club on base, and as we were riding along (my two girlfriends from Miami and two guys we met), I was in the front seat with the driver, and my friends were in the back. So, as we're riding along, I heard a voice say, "You know you're not supposed to be going there!" and I thought that was a strange statement considering we're all going out there together. I asked the driver, "What did you say?" He replied, "I didn't say anything." So as we're riding along, I heard it again, so again I asked, "What did you say? I know you said something!" and he replied, "I didn't say anything. I'm just listening to the music," and again the voice said, "You know you're not supposed to be going out there," so I turned around and said to Jetta, "Stop playing. I know that's you," and she said, "What are you taking about? I didn't say anything to you?" And as I took notice of how they were playing around in the back, I knew she was telling the truth.

Therefore, I sat there trying to figure out what was going on, thinking to myself saying, I know what I heard. I know I'm not crazy, but no one seems to know what I'm talking about. Still thinking "Who said that" and before I could finish my thought pattern, it looked as if the clouds opened and the moon shined on me, and I knew the voice. And before I knew it, I replied, "But God, I can't tell him to turn the truck around and say 'God doesn't want me to go to the club.'" The driver asked, "Are you okay?" I said yes! And it was like a broken record because he said the same thing! So I fixed my mouth to say, "Can you take me home because God doesn't want me to go to the club?" and when I looked at him to say it, I thought, Oh Lord, he's going to put me out of the truck on the side of the road. So I said to the angel of the Lord, If you get me through this night, I promise never to go to a club again.

I thought that night would go smoothly, but can I tell you the devil showed his behind in that place. It seemed like every man in there wanted to talk to me! Now, I was looking cute, I'll admit, but not for the attention I was getting. Even my friends were like, "Girl, what is going on!" I could be talking to one guy and look up, and another is trying to get my attention as if the other was not standing there! Another guy snatched me off the dance floor from dancing with another guy, saying he didn't like the way the other guy was rubbing up against me. You'd think I was a superstar the way some of them were acting! I was getting numbers left to right! I was walking out of the club and a guy was giving me his number, and soon as I got outside, another one handed me his number! My girlfriend asked, "Is it a full moon?" But in my mind, I'm thinking, I don't know, and I don't care. All smiles over here! (It was an illusion the enemy created as a distraction.)

The next day as I'm talking with one of the guys, I hear that voice again saying, "It doesn't matter how many numbers you get. You can only date one man at a time." I was like, What? And by end of the day, all the numbers were gone! It was like they vanished, never to be seen again, and I know because I looked all over the apartment for them. And for the record, these guys were fine, I mean very nice-looking men! When they say the devil knows what you like, they were not lying! I was like a kid in the candy store next to Baskin-Robbins!

See, the enemy heard me tell God I wasn't going back after that night, so what did he do? He sent out his best weapon, my weakness: Men—fine, good-looking men (chocolate, caramel, strawberry; short, tall, bearded, bald), and they looked like they had themselves together! Ooooh, the black man, the black man. God knew what he was doing when he created the black man. No disrespect to the other race, but OMG! Black men are simply beautiful to me! Okay, okay, focus! I thank God he's all-knowing because he alone knew what would have happened if he didn't intervene!

Even though I went back the other way for a season, the angel of the Lord was still with me!

One day at work while cleaning the rooms, I decided to watch television (normally I don't). Going from room to room, I put the TV on TBN. During this time, Pastor E. B. Hill was on and he was telling a story about a man that went to hell. I wasn't really bothered since I've heard this kind of story before—man going to hell, blah, blah, blah! Nevertheless, he talked about the different parts of hell and the different tortures the people were going through, but nothing seemed to make him pay attention. He was unbothered by the worms and snakes, crawling all over the people or hearing them scream out in pain. He said nothing worried him until he was leaving. He said as he turned around to leave, he saw his father standing there and was shocked to see that he was in hell! And in shock he asked, "What are you doing here? You're not supposed to be here!" Now, let me tell you, I have never been more afraid until I heard that. I stood there shaking, simply because in my mind I know *no* one wants to believe that their loved ones are in hell.

We hear it all the time when someone dies. "RIP. Oh, he/she's in a better place" or "Grandpa's watching over us from heaven" and "Big Momma's smiling down on us. Can't wait to see her again." But the question is, Are they? I was so scared I couldn't wait to go to church! I had a date that night, and when he came to pick me up, I asked him to take me to church. He looked at me like "Are you for real?" He was hesitant at first, but because I was so persistent, he decided to take me.

When I got to the church I ran to the door, and I stood there shaking it because it wouldn't open. I was confused! I started saying, "Hello, hello, I know someone's in there. It's Sunday night," but no one responded. My date shouted from the car, "There's no one in there!" but I didn't believe him. I said, "But it's Sunday night!" and I kept shaking the door thinking maybe it's just early so I'll wait for a little. But when I came to myself and looked around, I realized we were the only ones in the parking lot! I slowly walked back to the car, shaking my head in disbelief!

The Wattses used to pick me up on Sunday morning or I would take the church van, but since I started working every Sunday, I had to try and find a ride on Sunday night or Tuesday and Friday evenings!

Now I'm thinking, I need to find me another job because I couldn't keep missing church every Sunday! All I kept thinking about was that man's father being in hell, and that's not where I wanted to be!

I started working at major department store, and I was able to have some Sundays off. (I don't know if I could use their name so, I'll just say WM!) Nevertheless, every Sunday that I was off I went to church, and if I found a ride on Tuesdays or Friday, I went to Bible study, but I didn't stop there. The Potters' house was up to the street from where I lived up on Lane Avenue and their services were on Wednesday evening, so I would walk up the street and sit in on their Bible study! I was on a mission to know this God I was serving. And the more I grew, the more I wanted to share the gospel with others!

I turned my job into a ministry! Every time a Disney movie came out, my job would give us these pins to put on our smock for advertisement. One day I decided to alter the pins. The first one I covered said, "Smile, Jesus loves you," then I started putting scriptures on them, and as people came through my line, they would always pause from what they were doing to read them. My vest was full! Some people would just stare, some would smile, and some said thank you! Every now and then, I'd hear someone say, "That's my favorite scripture." In addition to that, some would ask for prayer! Some of them I would pray for right on the spot, and others I'd pray for when I got home. I even came across an atheist who tried to challenge my belief, but I was too far gone for them to come for me! I was on my mission to tell everyone I met about Jesus!

I remember this one lady. She was tall and had light complexion, and her hair was red (blonde). It was around the Christmas holidays. She came through my line because she forgot something the first time she was there. She said to me, "I feel so bad; I was in here earlier and I was complaining about what I couldn't buy, and I had a cartful. But I looked over at you, and you were smiling. And I'm thinking with all these people in here, she must be tired, but she had this big smile on her face like she doesn't have a care in the world, and you're still smiling." Then she took notice of my vest and said, "Oh, I see why you're smiling!" All I could do was smile.

I met a lot of guys during this time, but in my "dating," I only had one serious relationship back then. However, I remember the voice of the Lord saying to me,

"The men that I bring into your life are for you to minister to, not for you to date!" At first, I was like, Seriously! Nevertheless, after that relationship ended, that's exactly what I did.

A friend of mine said she knew someone who was selling her car because she purchased another one and wanted to know if I would be interested in buying it, and I said, "Of course, I would!" I was excited about owning a car. So that week I talked to her and she sold it to me for $500! It was a tan, 1989 four-door Chevy Cavalier! I was so grateful to have a car. I didn't have to depend on anyone else for a ride. It was a newfound freedom! I drove that car until I couldn't drive it anymore!

After many years of service, that season had come to an end, and God blessed me with another job working at Insurance company working Monday to Friday! So now I have every Sunday off! Yay me! To God belongs all the glory! Not only was I attending church, but I was also able to get involved in the ministry like I wanted to!

I've learned so much sitting under this ministry throughout the years. God truly blessed me with great leaders! I may seem a little biased when I say that I have the greatest pastor and first lady on this side of heaven, but I do! God used them to minister to me in so many ways. I can't tell you how grateful I am. I still can't believe it's been more than twenty years!

CHAPTER 4

WORDS OF ENCOURAGEMENT

Never allow anyone to speak anything into your life that's contrary to the word of God. If God gave you a word, come hell or high water, you stand on it! The enemy will try to make you feel like God's word will not come to pass, but my question is, What did he say to you? Do you still believe it, or did you give up? I know it's hard when your reality doesn't line up with your faith! When you believe in God but can't find the silver lining in the cloud, "Write the vision, make it plain upon tables, that he may run that readeth it" (Hab. 2:2b).

Let me encourage you to keep a journal so when you get weary, or it looks like things are not working in your favor, you can go back and read what God said! And don't just read it once—read it over and over until it gets deep down in your soul. Keep in mind that some people will try to kill your hopes and dreams, but you can't let that stop you!

Wait . . . Stop . . . Listen . . . Can I tell you a secret? Shhhh! Okay, look to the left and right to see who might be listening to what I'm about to say! Is the coast clear? Good!

"You can't tell everyone what God told you, and you can't make people believe what God revealed to you!"

There, I said it! They're not going to understand or see things the way you do because the Spirit did not reveal it to them, so stop trying to convince the inconvincible! In addition to that, you must be mindful of that Delilah spirit—people that want you to tell them your secrets so they can kill your dreams. If you think I'm lying, ask Samson (Judges 16)!

Okay, so back to what I was saying . . . Be mindful. Death isn't always physical. God told Adam, "The day that you eat of this tree you shall surely die."

"And the woman said unto the serpent, We may eat of the fruit of the trees of the garden: But of the fruit of the tree which is in the midst of the garden, God hath said, Ye shall not eat of it, neither shall ye touch it, lest ye die" (Gen. 3:2) KJV

The day that you start believing what people speak over you that's not lined up with the word of God, you shall surely die! Remember that death and life are in the power of the tongue. *"Death and life are in the power of the tongue: and they that love it shall eat the fruit thereof" (Prov. 18:21). KJV*

Regardless if it's their tongue or yours! So again, be careful what you allow people to speak into your life! Whatever comes to your ear that's not lined up with the word of God should be rebuked in the name of Jesus. In addition, be very careful what you speak over yourself. It's important to understand the power of the tongue (power of *your* words). The Word also states that "Faith cometh by hearing and hearing the word of God"! Hearing what? "Words." So again I encourage you to *speak life*!

No matter how gloomy your situation may look, I don't care if they already had the funeral, or if someone is telling you it's too late! I don't care what you're believing God for. If he made you a promise, then (his word) *trust* me, it isn't over until God says it's over! He can resurrect *any* situation! Remember the story of Lazarus.

"Then when Jesus came, he found that he had lain in the grave four days already . . . Then said Martha unto Jesus, Lord, if thou hadst been here, my brother had not died. But I know, that even now, whatsoever thou wilt ask of God, God will give it thee. Jesus saith unto her, Thy brother shall rise again. Martha saith unto him, I know that he shall rise again in the resurrection at the last day. Jesus said unto her, I am the resurrection, and the life: he that believeth in me, though he were dead, yet shall he live" (John 11:17, 21–25, KJV).

Contrary to what you might think, everyone does not hate you. There are some people standing in the gap and going to God on your behalf. Things may appear to be dead, but there's a resurrection coming! God is about to raise you *up*! Now take a minute and tell him thank you! Clap your hands, open your mouth, and give him *Shabach* praise! Hallelujah!

CHAPTER 5

FLASHBACK

There is an old saying and it is still prevalent today! We do not always have to make our own mistakes to learn a lesson; we can also learn from the mistakes of others. Life can teach us lessons in so many ways, but we must be willing to hear what the Spirit is saying to us. You don't have to text and drive to get into an accident to know that you shouldn't text and drive. You can look at the news and see what's going on and notice that a lot of people are dying because of texting and driving, so why wouldn't you want to stop! You don't have to smoke to know that it can cause damage to your lungs or cause cancer. There are billions of commercials talking about what smoking can do to you if you start or don't stop!

I remember watching a video in junior high school; it was a video of a woman who was on drugs. It talked about all the damage drugs caused and how it can affect you. They showed the before and after pictures, and I was like, Woohoo, she looked horrible! I was terrified; I said I know I will not be doing drugs if I could end up looking like that! Then there was a time we took a field trip to the jailhouse in downtown Miami. The way some of those men were acting when we walked in there scared the crap out of me. They were jumping on bars, screaming and pointing at us, saying, "I want you. I want you." We were scared to death! There was no way I was going to jail if I could help it! I was too horrified at what could happen to me. Now you see, there are some things in life we can learn from without going down the same path to prove a point.

I said all that to say this, listen to your parents, young people! I know sometimes you think you know it all, and think they don't know anything because they're, as you put it, "old," and you say it's a new day and they don't know what they're talking about, but trust me when I tell you they do! Contrary to what you may think, you don't know more than your parents, and yes, some of you may be a little smarter, but you're not wiser. Therefore you still don't know more than they do. Total difference.

When I was sixteen, my best friend and I always wanted to be around each other. We didn't care if it was for five minutes or five hours. We did just about everything together. On this day, she wanted to hang out after school, but my mom told us earlier not to leave the house. Hmm, what's a girl to do? Well, I told her I couldn't come to her house so what we decided to do was to meet up for a few minutes. We met up at the halfway point then walked around and talked about whatever came to our minds.

Now on the way home, I ran into this guy (let's call him Dee). He was tall with a caramel complexion; a handsome young man. He always used to flirt with me, but at the time I was not allowed to date, so that's as far as it would go. He would always say, "I have a crush on you. Too bad I can't drink you!" (the Crush soda was popular back in the eighties) and I would always laugh. He asked if he could walk me home, and I said yes because he's done it before; however, he would walk me to the corner of Forty-ninth and Miami because boys weren't really allowed to come to the house.

Nevertheless, we headed home, and he suggested we take the shortcut through the school. Not a problem; we did it all the time. Besides, I knew him, so I thought nothing of it! So we walked and talked. I laughed at a few of his jokes, no biggie, but by the time we got to the exit, which was by the front of the cafeteria, I felt my feet leave the ground, and before I knew it, I reached up and grabbed the fence thinking, What in the world is going on. I have to say it caught me off guard, yet he was pulling me as hard as he could. Again I'm thinking what is going on and I screamed out, "Put me down! Put me down!" but he wouldn't! I held on to that fence for as long as I could, until I couldn't hold on to it anymore. Then he picked me up and carried me to the other side of the cafeteria.

I could feel the leaves and rubble from the cherry trees rubbing against my skin, and I was still screaming, "What are you doing? Why are you doing this?" As I lay there screaming, begging him to stop, I could hear people in the distance. I could hear children playing, and I could hear people laughing, but no one heard my screams! Now I'm thinking to myself, I can hear them; why can't they hear me! When he put his hand around my throat and threatened to kill me if I didn't shut up, it was like my soul left my body at that moment. The fear that entered me took me to a place I've never experienced before in my life. I whispered, "How can you do this and why are you doing this to me?! Please don't!" With one hand, he held me down and with the other he removed my clothes. Lying there, I said to him, "I thought you were my friend. Like how can you do this? I thought we were friends!" But he was like, "If you don't shut up, I will kill you!" So, at this point, he seemed to be believable, but I still cried, begged, and pleaded with him to stop but he didn't.

Afterward he got up and he left me there and I lay there for only God knows how long before I got up and started to head home before I realized that I didn't have on any clothes so I turned back around thinking, "What will I tell my mother if I walked into the house naked?" Bad enough I left the house when I should have stayed home. I went back to find my clothes and put them on. Walking out of the school, still hurt and in disbelief, I could still hear the people laughing in the distance, and I was still thinking to myself, How's it that I can hear them, but they couldn't hear me! I was mad, I was upset, and I was hurt! I was walking in a daze! When I passed by Omar's house, I heard a voice ask, "Are you okay?" And I whispered, "Yeah," and kept going. I don't know if it was him or his dad sitting outside because I didn't even look up to see who it was. I couldn't stop. I didn't want him to know what had happened. As a matter of fact, I didn't want anyone to know what had happened!

When I got home, I headed straight to the bathroom, ran a hot bath, and got in the tub. I stayed there for the longest. I started examining all the scratches and bruises on my body, thinking how I was going to explain this! Oh, that's right, I don't! I'll just cover it up! Afterward I got out of the tub and got into my bed and went to sleep and there I buried the memory of that night! (After all, he said if I told anyone, he would kill me.) Oh, the secrets that we keep! I remember sitting in that tub thinking, How could this have happened to me? Why, God? Why me? Being disobedient, some might say yes! Well, I lived with that guilt all my life, being reminded that the first time a man touched me, I was raped! What an awful feeling. For a few years, I would have nightmares. Every year around the time it happened, I would dream that he was chasing me, and I ran tirelessly in fear of him catching me and hurting me again. I would wake up screaming, scared to go back to sleep because I knew he would be waiting for me! I didn't realize that even though it was buried, it was still affecting my relationships.

I know it's never easy reliving the past, but talking about it does help with the healing process. So, let's take a break and say a prayer, if not for me or you, but for someone you know that's been through something like this. The way I knew I was not totally healed was when I was uncomfortable talking about it! But believe me when I tell you, I'm not where I used to be! I used to be in a room with people talking about their experience, and I would just look on and shake my head, never showing any emotions because I still didn't want anyone to know what I'd been through! Well, let us *pray*!

Father, I pray for the person reading this that was affected by molestation or rape in any way, form, or fashion. Give them the mind to understand it was not their fault. I know they can't go back to the future and change the past, but they can look to the future and declare that they are healed from all the hurt and pain that was afflicted upon them by the hands of the enemy. Give them the strength to face the demons in their minds and be able to cast down every imaginations according to 2 Corinthians 10:5 (KJV): *"Casting down imaginations and every high thing that exalteth itself against the knowledge of God, and bringing into captivity every thought to the obedience of Christ."* Lord, we know that there is nothing too hard for you; therefore I ask that you would allow healing to take place in our lives right now. In Jesus's name. Amen!

Okay, after that I need a break, so let's take one. Below you will find a puzzle that I put together. Let's see how many words you can find. J

```
J  O  Y  F  U  L  L  F  I  L  L  E  D  Y  S  A  V  E  D
B  A  N  K  I  S  S  A  P  H  E  R  R  T  P  G  I  K  A
A  O  V  I  S  U  A  L  R  V  C  O  E  I  I  E  O  S  N
H  S  A  L  V  A  T  I  O  N  A  T  A  N  R  N  L  A  C
A  H  C  A  K  E  S  L  M  E  E  S  M  U  I  D  I  U  E
M  S  A  D  S  A  A  Y  I  V  P  E  F  T  T  A  N  G  O
A  E  T  Y  J  E  S  U  S  E  A  R  A  R  Z  S  N  U  W
S  L  I  A  R  G  T  Q  S  R  X  O  M  O  N  I  O  S  L
U  F  O  O  Q  F  R  E  E  T  I  P  I  P  A  M  I  T  G
Y  K  V  I  C  T  O  R  Y  H  H  E  L  P  D  P  T  A  N
Z  A  C  T  I  O  N  I  C  E  P  A  Y  O  I  L  A  K  I
F  A  S  T  I  N  G  O  D  L  Y  K  A  O  R  I  C  E  D
A  F  O  R  G  I  V  E  N  E  S  S  Y  L  O  C  A  R  D
C  R  U  C  I  F  I  E  D  S  T  A  N  D  L  I  V  S  E
N  E  I  G  H  B  O  R  S  E  A  S  O  N  F  T  A  H  W
W  A  N  N  I  V  E  R  S  A  R  Y  N  A  V  Y  M  R  A
```

CHAPTER 6

SOUND THE ALARM

As life went on, it brought about a change I didn't expect or saw coming. The hurricanes that came into my life left a lot of broken pieces. Like I stated earlier, everything that I thought could go wrong did, but through it all God kept me!

You know the saying, "Warning goes before destruction" Well, I can't say God didn't prepare or alerted me to it. He sounds the alarm, and in the midst of it he said, "Trust me!"

Here's the preparation:

"The Lord is my light and my salvation; whom shall I fear? The Lord is the strength of my life; of whom shall I be afraid? When the wicked, even mine enemies and my foes, came upon me to eat up my flesh, they stumbled and fell. Though a host should encamp against me, my heart shall not fear: though war should rise against me, in this will I be confident. One thing have I desired of the Lord, that will I seek after; that I may dwell in the house of the Lord all the days of my life, to behold the beauty of the Lord, and to inquire in his temple. For in the time of trouble he shall hide me in his pavilion: in the secret of his tabernacle shall he hide me; he shall set me up upon a rock. And now shall mine head be lifted up above mine enemies round about me: therefore will I offer in his tabernacle sacrifices of joy; I will sing, yea, I will sing praises unto the Lord (Psalms 27:1–6 KJV).

For the most part, the Lord deals with me in dreams, so for me, I would write them in my journal, where I wake up and can go back and read over them later, to get a better understanding. However, this dream was different. It was preparing me for what was to come. It was like watching my life on a movie screen!

Dream: We were at a church function like the Holy Convocation, and all the leaders were there. Bishops from all over the state were there. The bishop was up speaking, and the place was crowded. There was a lot of people still coming in trying to find seats. There was a seat next to me, so I alerted the usher to inform her. The service was hype, and the bishop was walking down the aisle, laying hands on the people as he was preaching. (Not the norm for him.) Then he laid his hands on me, and when he touched me, I fell to the floor but got up in the spiritual realm on the other side.

I could feel a presence all around me—spiritual beings (a little frightful)! I heard a voice say, "Trust me," so I started thanking God and praising him and telling him that I trust him in response to what he was saying to me. Afterward, I started floating with my body looking upward, moving as if someone was carrying me, but I couldn't see them! Now I'm in a bedroom lying on a bed looking around trying to take in everything around me but continuing to praise God! As I was praising God and talking to him again, this presence was all around me. It was fearful, but I felt peaceful at the same time. It reminds me of Daniel in chapter 10 when he was kneeling before the angle.

I noticed the curtains on the windows. They were yellow and white, and I said, "Wow!" Yellow and white curtains. There was something that stood out about them, but the yellow one really got my attention because it illuminated the room. They were moving like the wind was softly pushing them. The room was bright and calm, and outside was like a bright and sunny day. The grass was evergreen, and the trees in the distance stood still. Then after that, I was floating again and now I'm in what looks like an elevator going up slowly, but the doors were open. When it stopped, I saw what looked like a man standing off in a corner, a tall and black shadow. He looked as if he was watching me, but he didn't move.

As I stood there, I felt a push and now I'm falling, and as I was falling, I was looking upward, and the image that was watching me in the corner was now watching me as I was falling, but now there's two of them. I was not afraid. (Okay, a little.) I was trying to make out what they were but couldn't. Again, they were both tall, 7 or 8 feet, give or take, not just black but "shadow black," and as I focused on them, I noticed the muscles in their legs looked like horse legs. Their top part, waist up, looked human, except for their face! It was like nothing I've ever seen before, not even in the movies! I didn't know what they were, but I know they were not human! I don't want to call them a demon, but I'm sure they were not angels! Yet, as I was falling, it felt like someone was holding me the entire time because I was falling in slow motion. The only reply to the voice I heard was "Lord, I trust you!"

"Now unto him that is able to keep you from falling, and to present you faultless before the presence of his glory with exceeding joy" (Jude 1:24). KJV

When I woke up, I said, "Lord, have mercy!" What was that! I began to pray and asked God to reveal to me what this dream was all about! He opened my understanding but did not go into a lot of details. He also said to not be alarmed and that I was to "trust him."

To me, dreams are not just dreams. I believe a great percentage of my dreams have hidden messages. Sometimes direct, and sometimes they're like putting a puzzle together. Some dreams deal with my present state, others about my future, so I don't take them lightly!

I felt like Peter in Luke 22:33, screaming, "Pray for me too, Jesus!"

"And the Lord said, Simon, Simon, behold, Satan has desired to have you, that he may sift you as wheat. But I have prayed for thee, that thy faith fails not; and when thou art converted strengthen thy brethren" (Luke 22:31, NKJ).

Life happens; the storms will come but thank God for his backup team that's always ready—the Father's Emergency Medical Angels (FEMA). They came in and ministered to me when I need them the most. One thing about God, he'll never leave you comfortless. Yes, it might feel like it at times, but be assured he is always there.

The word reminds us "that they that live holy will suffer persecution."

CHAPTER 7

IN MY FEELINGS

I hate when people say, "Girl, you don't want to get married. It's hard work," or "You don't want to have children—borrow mine!" What the heck does that mean? I'm sorry, are you the only one strong enough to get married, or are you the only one who's supposed to have children? And why do I need to borrow your children, and is your husband on layaway too? I think not! Besides, you might want to keep little Johnny home! It's like they say, I'm not going to treat him the way you would. If he gets out of line with you, you might baby him. If he gets out of line with me, I'm taking him to the throne room, you feel me. Pop-pop, you know the rest! So umm . . . no, thank you, I'll pass!

Don't get me wrong, I know what some of them were trying to say, but that's not what God's words say. In life, there are lessons to be learned, I get it. Some we can learn by watching what we see others go through, and there are lessons you must learn on your own in order to build character, independence, reliance, and self-respect. There are just some things you must go through in life. I know you think your marriage is the bomb because you've been married on paper for over twenty years, but you've only been committed for five so go have a seat, Felicia! Bye! Rolling my eyes!

Let them not get married, or not have children based on what God's plan is for their life, not your opinion or what you assume for their life. No, not everyone will get married or even have children. I get that, trust me, I do, but let that be their decision, not yours! Consequently, you will never understand the pain in someone's heart who has a desire to have children and not be able to! Oh, and another thing, stop telling women they're too old to have children in their forties! Please stop being so insensitive. Yes, we know the risk could be a little higher than the norm, but with the proper diet and exercise, a woman in her forties can still have a healthy baby! I see it all the time. So again, please stop being so insensitive. Y'all really don't know the pain behind someone's smile. Besides, God can do anything!

Hey, I said I was in my feelings, but I'm okay, I'm done, so let's move on!

CHAPTER 8

WHAT'S IN A NAME

When I lived at home, I used to love to sit and listen to my mother pray. Sometimes when I came home from the club, she would still be up, and I would sit by her door and just listen. (Yeah, I said club.) Her faith was so strong! Regardless of what she was going through or how things looked, she did not stop praying. She trusts and believes in the God she served. This is one of the reasons my prayer life is what it is today. I had a strong foundation. Nevertheless, one night when she was visiting me, she was in her room praying, and like at home, I was in my room listening! I went into her room and asked her to pray for me.

I was so excited. I sat there anticipating a move of God, and she began to pray. She said, "Lord, bless August Kelly," and before I knew it, I stopped her! I said, "No, no, that's not my name." Then she replied, "Well, you know what I mean," but I said, "Yeah, but that's not what you said!" At the time my husband and I were separated, so I really needed her to be in faith with me. I know it might sound like a small thing, but spiritually it's not. Remember, "Death and life are in the power of the tongue." Don't allow people to keep you in your past and call you what you used to be. That's like someone sending mail to your old address! You don't live there anymore!

I have a friend, and her name is Erica. When she got married, we were all happy and excited for her. Oh my! One day as were standing around talking, one of the sisters came up and started talking to her. As they were talking, however, another young lady came up and interrupted her, and this is how that conversation went.

Lisa: Hey, Sis. Simmons!

With no hesitation, Erica replied, "Harris," and continued conversing with the person she was talking to!

Lisa: Sis. Simmons . . .

Erica: Harris [Kept on talking.]

Lisa: Oh, girl, you know what I meant!

As we walked away, Regina and I started laughing, but Erica said jokingly and sarcastically, "She knows my name is now Harris," and we started laughing!

I didn't think much of it at the time other than it was a good laugh, but looking back now, I totally get what she was saying. In other words, she was letting her know, "I'm no longer single. I am *married*! My name has changed." Now, some might think that's not a big deal, but the truth of the matter is, it really is a *big* deal! First natural, then spiritual!

CHAPTER 9

MY NAME IS NOT SARAH

One of the worst feelings in the world is to feel like there's something growing inside of you and knowing that nothing's there. That feeling is so painful. It's not just mental or physical, but it was also emotional and indescribable. I've always wanted to have children, but I wanted to wait until I was married. By the time I got married, I was thirty-nine, However, I still wanted to wait a year before we start trying to conceive because I didn't want to start a family at the beginning of our marriage. I wanted to spend time with my husband and get to know him.

After a year we decided to try and conceive. Despite my age (forty at the time), I was still looking forward to motherhood. After trying for months, we were unsuccessful. I can recall how my mind used to play tricks on me! Once I didn't have my menstrual period for two months, so in my mind, I just knew I was pregnant. In my excitement, I went and purchased a pregnancy test. The first test came back not pregnant, so I took it again thinking, "I know I'm pregnant!" The second test came back *not* pregnant, so now I'm scheduling an appointment with my OB-GYN. After all, I had no menstrual cycle for a few months, but again, I got the same answer! I had to fight back the tears because I was so disappointed, trying so hard to get pregnant but to no avail.

My GYN set up an appointment for me to have a biopsy of the uterus and then scheduled me for a vaginal ultrasound and CT scan. I then discovered that I had multiple fibroids, which hinder my chances of getting pregnant; I knew I had like one or too, but it was like over ten! In addition to that, she also stated that my egg count was low. According to my OB-GYN, removing the fibroids would increase the chance of conception so I decided to have them removed through a procedure called a myomectomy that she recommended. The crazy thing about the fibroids was at times when they would move, it felt like there was a baby moving inside of me. So naturally at times I would think I was pregnant. I know it might sound crazy, but that's how I felt.

Now that the fibroids are removed, we are at it again trying to get pregnant. Unfortunately, we are still unsuccessful. Afterward, I went months with no menstrual period to every other month. Then I would have it only two to three days to only twenty-four hours, to nothing! (I wasn't mad.)

My ex-husband would say, "I want a son. Don't you want a chocolate baby? Don't you want a son? I think you would make a great mom!" and I would just look at him thinking, "If I answer this man, I am going to break down and cry." The pain was too much to deal with, so I would just smile and brush it off, and change the subject, if you will. Understanding it was harder on me because I didn't have any children.

One night in bed, I explained to him how I felt about not being able to give him a child (son, as he would put it, since he already had two girls) and how painful it was for me to talk about it, but he was thinking I didn't want a child because I would always laugh it off. I had to inform him I just didn't want to deal with the pain of not being able to conceive.

I'll admit I was a little upset (no, a lot!) with God. Talking to God and thinking, Look at all the people in the world that have children and abuse them, or women getting pregnant and have abortions, in addition to the drug babies being born and being taken away from their mothers. Or the countless teenage pregnancies (no disrespect) thinking, I waited! I did what you said to do, how you said to do it, and still came up short and empty. Yep, it looks like I've gotten the short end of the stick. I couldn't tell you how many pregnancy tests I took—two or three times a month, hoping and praying maybe this time it would be positive! Looking for that plus (+) sign!

Thinking back, I recalled an incident that happened to me in elementary school. One day I was playing on the monkey bars and I fell, both legs opposite of the bars, and it caused me to bleed as if I was having a menstrual cycle. So my parents took me to the doctor to get it checked out. I can remember the doctor saying something about it affecting me in the future if something wasn't done. A couple months later, I got into a confrontation with some girls after school and one of them punched me in the back and immediately I started bleeding again. I can't help but wonder if this also played a part in me not being able to conceive. Just a thought!

Mother's Day was one of the worst celebrated days for me. People would always recognize you "as a mother figure" if you played a role in a child's life—godmother, stepmother, auntie, mentor—but it wasn't the same. There was always that emptiness, that loneliness, the longing of feeling that child grow inside of you, wanting to know what it felt like to feel that first kick (some might feel it's overrated), but that's how I felt. There will be no first birthday, first day of school, no sweet sixteen. Prom night and graduation are out of the question. No boys or girls to fight off, no chance of being the mother of the bride or groom, and no kissing the grandchildren good night. Or the worst ever, who's going to take care of me when I'm old or bury me when I die. I know that last one sounded a little harsh, but that's a reality check for me. I know the insurance will pay for the burial, but for me, the nursing home will be my residence until my departure! Again, if you have children, you will never understand the pain and the void of barrenness. I was always happy to celebrate everyone else, but I still was feeling empty inside!

Sometimes people would refer to me as Sarah because of my age! They would say "Well, Sarah was old when she had Isaac, so there's still hope for you," but I would always reply, "Well, my name is not Sarah!" And if that wasn't bad enough, it was "Are you sure you want a baby at your age?" (You would think I was seventy-five going on one hundred the way some people were talking!) I know they meant well, but sometimes people really need to think before they speak. (And it was always the people who had children that were the most insensitive!) I would always say, "Age is not a factor when God is in control." Unfortunately a baby was not in the cards for me, but I had to remind myself that God is too wise to make a mistake. It didn't stop the way I felt, and there were many nights I cried myself to sleep in silence because it was too painful to deal with. Nevertheless, I trust God's plan for my life.

CHAPTER 10

HOW WE MET

I remember the first time I saw Mr. The Singles Ministry went down to dancing in the street (line dancing) on Riverside. I didn't know what to expect or much about line dancing, but when we got down there, I knew it was something I would be interested in participating in. It was crowded and everyone seemed to be having a good time. Funny thing though, as much as I love to dance, the only line dance I knew was the electric slide (hahaha), so I just stood around and watch. After standing for so long, I decided to take a seat and rest my nerves. Then after sitting there for a few, still watching the people dancing, it looked as if the crowd parted like the Red Sea and there he was dancing. He caught my attention right away, so I sat up thinking, "Now who is this young man." He was a chocolate brother with a fresh haircut and nicely dressed. His dancing skills were on point, and he was smooth with it and sexy too! I was impressed.

There was just something about him that stood out from the rest of everyone else out there. I couldn't put my finger on it, but like I said, he caught my attention right away, and I could not shake him; he was like glue on my mind. I thought about him all night. There was no one I knew that knew him so I couldn't inquire about him. I couldn't wait to go back. I had to meet him! Who is he? What is his name? I wanted to know if he was single or involved, or is he married? *What*?! I had nothing! When I got home, I called my best friend who lived in Georgia at the time and I said, "Regina, I think I saw my future husband," and we both laughed. (Yeah, I know it's he that finds a wife.)

We went back the following Friday, and yes, my sole purpose was to see him again. And yes, I was infatuated! I wanted to get to know him. The following weekend Regina came to town for my birthday, and we went down there once again because I wanted her to see him. Mind you, I haven't said one word to him, just watching or should I say looking on from a distance. He was there every Friday night, and I was there to watch him, I meant, dance.

One night I got there a little early because I was meeting up with my girl Raya. Not too much going on, so I decided to wait by the light pole so she could see me when she got there. Guess who walked by as I was standing there? Yep, you guessed it, he did! He looked me right in my face, but I looked away trying to play it off, but by the end of the night, we were singing a different song.

It's the end of the night, and we were getting ready to leave, and as we were packing up, I noticed him standing behind us. The butterflies jumped in my stomach, and my chair dropped to the ground. Before I knew it, I asked him to pick it up. We exchanged a few words and I left. I must have left an impression because he caught up with us and asked for my name. We continue to converse and then walked Raya to her car, and he walked me to my car, and we stood there and talked for a while.

We exchanged numbers, and he asked me to call him the following night and I did. We talk briefly and said good night. A week went by, but neither of us reached out to each other. The following Saturday was Linda's wedding, so Drea, Regina, Tika, and I went to celebrate her special day with her. We had a great time, by the way!

By the time I got home and undressed, the phone rang and it was him. I excused myself for a little privacy and left the ladies to continue conversing among themselves. We talked for a little over an hour. We talked about our foundation, hobbies, and whatnots. I learned that he loved to cook and sing.

When we first started talking, I was all about him. I was at a place where I was ready to settle down but not rushing it. I asked of his expectations, and I told him of mine. However, when I told him that I was celibate, he advised that we could only be friends because he was not dating someone he couldn't sleep with, and I was cool with that because I was not dating anyone I had to sleep with before I was married! So, friends it was!

He would call and we'd chat with each other from time to time, and that was cool. What was not cool was I started dreaming about him, like all the time. It was like every other night. That to me was crazy because I never dreamed about anyone the way I dreamed about him. I would call Regina and Sandra and be like, "What do you think this means?" And they would say, "Look, girl, just pray about it!"

As if I wasn't already! Nevertheless, Regina advised me to talk to my pastor, and at first, I was like, "Nooooo way, Jose! That's not going to happen! What else you got?" However, I did pray about it, but I kept dreaming about him, and I wasn't getting the answers I was looking for. Now the dreams I was having were not the norm. These dreams were of the future of us being together. And they were in stages like him coming to my house for the first time.

#Pause Now. When he first came to my house, he said, "Wow, I've been here before!" I asked, "What do you mean?" and he said he dreamed about my house more than once, that everything was as it was in the dream, but he never saw who the person was!

Now back to what I am saying! Again, dreaming about him coming over to my house or us going out on dates, to just sitting around talking, all in my dreams. I kept a journal of all the dreams I had about him. Reading over them, I had mixed emotions because at this point, I really didn't know what to think. Yes, I prayed and prayed and prayed, but the more I prayed, the more I dreamed. Now I'm starting to stress a little because I felt like I was getting nowhere. There was a part of me that really believed this man was my husband, and the other praying, "God, I don't want to be misled or make a mistake, so please answer my prayer."

I stopped calling him because I really needed to clear my head to see what was going on. Sometimes I didn't want to sleep because I knew he was going to be waiting for me on the other side. So, months later, I took the advice of my friend and set up an appointment with my pastor to get some spiritual advice, hoping he could share some light on the situation. After all, he hears from God, right!

I don't know about you, but it is never easy going into my pastor's office to talk to him about anything. I always felt like I was going to the principal's office. Not that I had anything to hide. It was just a feeling, like God was going to tell him everything I did! Ha! Still, I sat there telling him everything I was feeling and all the dreams I was having about Mr., so he sat there listening, tapping his fingers on his desk, sounding like the four horsemen, then looked up to heaven and said, "Well, Sister Love, sometimes God speaks to us in dreams," then he pulled out his Bible and turned to Job and read chapter 33:14–16: *"For God speaketh once, yea twice, yet man perceiveth it not. In a dream, in a vision of the night, when deep sleep falleth upon men, in slumberings upon the bed; Then he openeth the ears of men and sealeth their instruction." KJV*

He said, "Sometimes God waits for us to go to sleep in order to get our attention." Then he went on to say, "I'm not saying it's something, and I'm not saying it's

37

nothing, but it's worth finding out. Why not call him up and invite him out to dinner and talk to him, not so much about the dreams because you don't want to run him away, but feel him out and see where his head is." Even though I heard all of that, my mind was still playing, "Invite him out to dinner!" I'm not going to lie to you, but I was not feeling that at all. I said to myself, "Forget it!" Besides, the Bible does say, "he that finds a wife." Maybe God will say something to him and he'll reach out to me! I was restless the next few days because I didn't want to do it.

Fast forward three days later on the way to work, I decided to give him a call. Butterflies are everywhere! We chatted for a few and then I got up the nerve to ask him out. I said, "Hey, maybe when you're not busy, we can go out and get something to eat." Do you know what he said to me? "Oh, I'm seeing someone!" I was thinking, "What the . . . *what*, what?" Already, because he was just single! I then said, "Hey, no problem. If you're seeing someone, then don't worry about it!"

Now you can imagine what's going through my mind. Yeah, "Why did I listen to my pastor?" I should have just left it alone. I felt so stupid! But here's the crazy part. After I calmed down, I said to myself, "It's not going to last because he's my husband." I felt it so strongly! I even called Regina and Sandra and told them about it! I just had this knowing that was unshakeable.

Months go by and he calls me up to "check up" on me, as he puts it. So, we know where this conversation is going, right. That relationship was over! We started talking again, but I kept it in the friend zone regardless of my feelings for him. I still did not want to rush into anything because I knew where he stood on the celibacy act. I know it was not my place to try to convince or change him. That was God's job! He started coming around like in the dream, hanging out, cooking, spending time together. One evening I was taking my nieces and nephew to Chucky Cheese to have some pizza and fun, so since he had his daughter for the summer, I invited them to come along with us. At this moment there was some bonding going on. However, that was short-lived because he disappeared *again*!

Months go by again, and he shows back up! Now at this point I am going through the motions because he shows back up wanting to hang around, cooking, and wanting to spend time with me. A part of me was thinking, "Maybe God is working on him" because he's acting like he wants to take it further, but at the same time he's stagnant. As before, no rush on my part, but I felt the strings of the yo-yo! Then, one day I decided to call him up and ask him, "What do you want from me?" And his reply was, "I don't know. Let me call you back." So now I'm playing the waiting game, waiting for the phone to ring! Finally, he calls back a few days later with the casual conversation as if he forgot what we were talking about. I politely asked him, "Are we going to talk about this?" And he said to me, "I don't want to put all of my eggs in the same basket." Hmmm! I'm confused! What eggs, what basket? Explain! So, he goes on to say, "I want to be with you, but I can't be with someone I can't sleep with! I need to think about this, I'll call you back!" A week went by, and I didn't hear from him. When he did finally call, he said he wanted to come over so that we could spend some time together! Did he show up? Of course not. He opted to call instead, telling me he had to go to a friend's funeral! Okay, I get that, but he still could've come over afterward! Besides, I cooked! So yeah, I was a little upset!

Seven days is what I told myself! I gave him seven days to contact me, and if he didn't, I was done trying to figure him out! Life went on as usual. After a while he started calling again. Sometimes I would answer, but I was very short with my words, and other times I would let it go to voicemail because I didn't want to talk to him. I was pretty much done.

A few months or so later I'm logging in online and checking my email, and guess what pops up? An IM from Mr. talking about how much he misses talking to me and hanging out with me, blah, blah, blah . . . I said okay and then logged off! I honestly didn't want to hear it!

The following night, I'm online minding my business, and I get another pop-up! I'm like, "Dang, how does he know I'm online?!" (Yahoo!) Nevertheless, he proceeded to say, "I was telling you how I felt last night and you didn't say anything," and I replied, "That's because you were expressing how *you* felt. That had nothing to do with me!" Now I'm getting ready to log off again, and he asked if I wanted to go see a movie. I did not reply. Then he said, "Hey, I'm taking my daughter to see *The Hulk*. Do you want to go?" So now I'm looking like, "He knows how I feel about that little girl. He's only using her as bait!" I felt numb, like I really didn't know that to do, so I called Regina and told her what had happened, and she said, "Girl, go!" and I was like, "No, I don't want to!" So, she put her big-sister hat on and said, "Girl, just go to the darn movie. It's not going to hurt you. It's just a movie." Meanwhile, he's still waiting for an answer.

I decided I'd go, but I'd meet him there. We decided to meet up on the southside. While in the theater, it was freezing like the North Pole, he asked if I was cold. I said no because I didn't want him touching me! I did notice him trying to get close, so I made sure I kept my distance. He called himself trying to hold my hands while exiting the theater, so I dropped my napkin on the ground and when he reached to pick it up, I put my hands in my pocket!

THE HOOK-UP

It's vacation time and I'm on the road to Atlanta. First stop: Macon, Georgia, to pick up the bestie (Regina) to head to Atlanta then off to Virginia to visit Erica and kin. Phone rings. I really don't feel like talking right now, so let's make this short! Hello! "It was nice seeing you. I miss hanging out with you," he said. "We need to talk about us . . . blah, blah, blah!" "Okay, well, I'm driving. Talk to you later. Goodbye." As I was heading into Macon, the phone rang again. "Did you make it there yet?" I gave him my ear and we talked for a few minutes or so while waiting for Regina to get in the car. I'm thinking, So what now? You're pursuing me? What's really going on?

I was up there for a week, and he called me every day. I'm talking three to four times a day! I couldn't tell you how many phone calls and text messages I got on that trip. You would have thought we were in a "relationship" but not. Now hear me when I say, at this point in my life I don't want to have anything to do with him. It's like suddenly you realize you want to be with me, and I really could care less.

However, it was on the way home that I appreciated his phone calls the most. Keep in mind, we drove straight from Virginia to Macon to drop Regina off and then I continue to Jacksonville by myself, so yeah, I was getting a little tired! However, I was doing fine until it started getting dark. I hate driving at night, and I started to get sleepy too. I called my friend Rob who lived in Seattle, Washington, to have someone to talk to, but he was at work and not available! I had to remind myself that we were in different time zones. If not, I would have been very upset. Now I'm driving down these dark Georgia roads wishing I had someone to talk to. I know Regina went to sleep so she was out of the question. My sister's best friend came to town that weekend, so she was entertaining a guest. I didn't think to bother anyone else, so I tuff it out, riding with music on blast!

I reached out to Bobby again, but he was still a little busy at work and couldn't talk, so again I had to take into consideration that he was in another time zone so I couldn't be too upset! Not long after I hung up from him, Mr. called. At that moment in time, I was so happy to hear his voice. We talked until his battery died, and then after a full charge he called me back and we talked until I made it home. I was beyond grateful for his help.

During our conversation, he invited me to a birthday dinner with some of his friends from church and a movie following. I was a little hesitant at first, but we went as friends. Yes, I placed a wall there because I didn't want to go back down that road again. Don't get me wrong, I still liked him as a person, but not someone I wanted to be with at the time.

Oh my, how the tables have turned! Now, I'm looking at my phone like really! I even got to the place where I was turned off by him. My sister and I would go to "dancing in the streets," and at this point, I know all the latest line dances! (Okay, dancing in the street was an event they had every Friday night during the summer on Riverside, right across from the Blue Cross building. People got together and did the latest line dances in the street. I didn't explain that earlier.) However, he would come over and speak, and I would speak back! Believe it or not, I can be very short with my words; my mother used to say I'm my father's child! Nevertheless, he would say hello, and I would say hi and I'll leave it there! At times I would look up and find him dancing next to me, and I'm like, "Where did he come from?" It was like he was doing any and everything to get my attention, but at this point, I'm in a different place. No, I wasn't trying to pay him back. I just wasn't feeling him the way I used to! I've moved on!

Now here is when things started to shift. I was in church one Sunday morning and as the pastor was preaching the message, he said, "God said, go at it again!" Hmm, in my mind I'm thinking he's not talking to me. And he said it again, "God said, go at it again!" This time I felt some type of way because I felt a little uneasy, so I said to myself, "Go at what again?" And when I thought it, Mr. popped up in my mind, and I said, "Oh no, God, I can't do that!" That can't be what he meant! So, I brushed it off. Then during Wednesday night's Bible study, the pastor said it again! "The Lord told me to pray and lay hands on everyone, and some of you need to go at it again." I was disturbed in my spirit.

I'm thinking there is no way in the world God is telling me to do that! After all I've been through, I'm done with it! Then he said, "God said to go at it like it was the first time!" I said, "God, I don't want to!" So as the line is moving, and Pastor Hall is praying and laying hands on the people. I'm crying out to God trying to figure out why would he want me to "go at it again"! I'm not going to lie to you, I cried because honestly at this point, I'm thinking I could do better. Then I thought, maybe I'm overreacting. That might not be what he meant at all!

As life went on, I was still in disbelief! I started praying and asking God for wisdom and understanding because I was going to need it! I did not rush into anything, but I kept telling myself, if this is really God, then he's going to make this happen as I prepare my mind to "go at it like it's the first time," and in the midst of that I kept praying!

He was consistent in his pursuit, but I was in no rush! He would call, and I would answer. He'd ask to come over, and I'd invite him. During our conversation I asked him, "What do you want?"

He answered, "You!"

"I said you do know I don't date for the sake of dating. I need to know where this is going."

"I know," he replied and just looked at me with this smile on his face! It was at this point where I agreed to courtship, and as we began to spend more time together, my feelings for him started to develop the more. "Look, at this point in my life, I don't have time for dating games." I mean I think every man over thirty-five, especially forty, should know what their relationship goals are!

There are just some things you need to know before you get into a relationship! If someone is not ready, respect their decision and remain friends. To answer the lifelong question: "Yes, a man and woman can be friends without strings attached," even if it started off with an attraction, but don't play the role of a hypnotist thinking you're going to change their minds, because, in the end, it might not work out in your favor.

Okay, I just had to pause and drop that in there. Forgive me for getting off track.

Let me also add, before I got saved or gave my life to Jesus, as some would put it, I too believed in the three-month rule, but now that I'm a believer, I implement the wedding-night rule. Because the truth of the matter is, I don't have to sleep with someone in order to know if I'm going to marry them. God's way is always right! Don't let the devil fool you into thinking you have to give up the goods for him to marry you! Personally, I believe this is one of the biggest lie men fall for, and some of their anticipation is like waiting for the results of an HIV test! Nerve-wracking! Instead of saying, "Let it be negative," they're saying, "Please let it be good, please let it be good, oh Laaaaawd, please let it be good!" There's this little thing called "self-control" that is lacking in so many peoples' lives, and I wish they'd take advantage of it.

Look, I just can't believe God could save me, deliver me, or heal me but don't believe he's able to bring someone into my life who's sexually compatible with me, even if it doesn't start off that way, because everything is workable if you're willing to work at it. If I did, that would mean my trust in him is limited. That's like me telling him, "God, I trust you for salvation, but let me pick my own mate.

I just need to test it out first!" How does that sound? Crazy, I know! You must have faith that God is able to do exceedingly and abundantly!

God is saying you want someone to please you, but you're not pleasing him. For without *faith*, it's impossible to please God. What if God said, well, until you learn to please him, he'll hold out on sending you someone to please you! I'm not going to limit God; therefore I'll wait.

THE PROPOSAL

He said, "What are you doing Saturday evening?" I said nothing. "Okay, don't make any plans. I'm taking you out!" Okay, cool. Saturday night dinner date around the Christmas holidays, my only question is, what am I going to wear? Something nice, of course! He was looking sharp when he came to pick me up. He had on his blue jeans, with a creamlike shirt with thin brown strips going down, a brown blazer to cover up, and his brown fedora. I, on the other hand, was wearing my black A-line dress with the gold spaghetti-like strap. The dress fit to the waistline and flowed a little at the hips. Casual conversation as we traveled along the way, a little laughter here and there; nothing special in the air, so I assume. Destination is Ruth's Chris on the river. Nice restaurant. I've been there a few times so I somewhat know what I wanted. As the night went on, we talked and laughed, just enjoying each other's company, but as it started to come to a close, he said, "I have something for you," so I'm looking like "For real?" because I didn't see him bring anything in. He then reached into his pocket and pulled out a ring! Now I'm like, "*What! Wait! What! You play too much . . .*" I just started laughing. (For the record, I have two emotions when I'm nervous: laugh or cry.) So he got up from his seat and got down on one knee and asked me to marry him. Meanwhile I'm still laughing in disbelief! So, after I stopped laughing and came to myself, I said yes!

OUR WEDDING DAY

I woke up to a beautiful day. The birds were singing, the sun was shining. Okay, there no were no birds singing. Truth be told, I was quite nervous. The butterflies started to kick in! But the sun was shining! Not too hot; just right. It felt perfect. I and a few of the bridal party went to Orange Park Mall to get our nails done, and after leaving there, we headed straight to the church. By the time we got there it was like a roller-coaster ride. Time just seemed to be moving too fast, and before we knew it, it was time to say, "I do!" The bridesmaids were going out and I was still not fully dressed. (That's because we started on time.)

Suddenly, I'm all alone, and now I'm getting nervous again. My shoe wouldn't stay on and I'm starting to freak out! The wedding coordinator's daughter came in to check on me, and she helped calmed me down. Now I'm waiting to walk out, but to what was the question! Now I'm standing at the door and the coordinator is telling me to go, and I'm looking at her like, "What song is that?!" When I heard his voice, I was like, OMG! Well, I said that because she and the groom were the only two that knew what song I was walking to because my ex wrote and sang the song. He wanted it to be a surprise, and it was. It was one of the only songs I didn't pick or approve for the wedding. The song was titled "A Thing of Beauty." It really is a beautiful song; you should take a listen if you need something to walk in on at your wedding!

As I walked down the aisle (I came in solo,) my dad met me halfway and walked with me the rest of the way! Why halfway, you ask? Well, with the rocky relationship we had, even though we were talking, he still found ways to get under my skin. Like even though he was invited, I didn't know if he was coming, because he never said that he was. And frankly, I didn't find out he was in town until the day of! Therefore, I had every intention of walking myself down that aisle. But I didn't allow pride to get in the way of what was supposed to have been my special day. I still allowed him the opportunity to give me away!

I didn't realize how many people were there until I looked at the pictures. Considering I'm the only one living in Jacksonville, I was blown away to see most of my family! They drove up from Miami in carloads; I was in awe of all the love and support they showed toward me!

The décor was simply beautiful. Purple silver and white were my colors (I love purple). Three shades of purple were the distinction between the matron of honor, maid of honor and bridesmaids, with silver shoes and accessories. The best men and groomsmen were all in black tuxedos with purple vest and silver ties. We were both in white! Everything was beautiful from what I saw because my focus was on him. I loved me some him!

The reception was laidback, but fun. Thanks to my boy, Freddy Mc., for being my DJ. (RIP, my love), to my big sister, Terecita, for catering—oh my goodness that food was delicious, and that cake from Publix was everything! Like I said, the day was perfect! Thanks to Gail and Jewel for taking on all the hard work.

CHAPTER 11

SOMETHING IS MISSING

As I stated in chapter 6 about "As life went on, life brought about a change I didn't expect or saw coming," and that "the hurricanes that came into my life left a lot of broken pieces." In addition, he had me scratching my head trying to figure out what went wrong. Well, as we go into the next few chapters, you'll understand why. Remember, some dreams are a sign of what's to come.

Okay, now according to the four gospels—Matthew, Mark, Luke, and John—they all walked with Jesus, but as you read the four gospels, you'll notice that they all saw things from a different perspective. Here, however, is my account of what took place in my marriage. Keep in mind, this is not to put him down or to make him look like less of a person. I'm just sharing my testimony.

I walked into work one day and was informed that a young man left a message for me to call him back. My coworker was a little surprised and wanted to know who the person was leaving me a message! She said, "Some guy name James called here for you," and asked me who he was. "Like I knew!" I replied. I don't know. But that look on her face said she wanted to know and so did I!

Now, because it was a man, I'm thinking, maybe he's calling to get his daughter, girlfriend, or maybe even his wife's hair done because I did get calls like that. Nevertheless, I called him back to see what he wanted. However, he proceeded to tell me that my husband and his wife were seeing each other. Stop, wait, hold the phones, *what*! At this point, I'm beside myself! He went on to say that she left her cell phone at home and he happened to see the text messages from Mr., and he decided "he" would reply to him. According to James, he decided to play along just to see where the conversation would go, and it went down the rabbit's hole. So now he's planning to meet up with "her" after choir rehearsal, or so he thought! After so many text messages between the two of them, he decided to confront Mr., because he couldn't take it anymore, and when he did, they exchanged unpleasant words. Mind you, I'm still trying to figure out how he got my name and work number, so I interrupted his thoughts and asked him! He stated he was so upset, he looked him up on Facebook to see who he was and when he got on Mr.'s page, he saw that he was "also married" and that's how he got my information. (Well, I'll be George!) And if that wasn't enough, he sent me all the text messages that were exchanged between the two of them—very disturbing!

Now, I'll be honest and say that this isn't the first time I had to deal with Mr.'s indiscretion, like the time he left his Facebook open and I read all of the messages he was sending to different women, telling them how beautiful they were and if things were different, he would be with them or the pictures he sent that were taken in my living room. No, I didn't take into consideration the many nights he was late coming home from rehearsal, and no, I didn't know he slept with someone else during our marriage until "I knew" he slept with someone else during the marriage! Got it? Okay, let's move on. But at this point, I honestly thought we were past that. I thought that my marriage was back on the right path. Not that we didn't have problems because we all do. We hit a few bumps in the road along the way, took some detours because of some constructions, but I thought our destination was the same. As he would put it, "You have me for forty years. After that we can renegotiate the contract!" Again, that's what he would always say. Besides, marriage is work! But I thought we were getting better in this department.

My mind is now racing a hundred miles with thoughts going left, right, horizontal, and vertical. I was thinking, "Is this it?! Is this the end of the road?" Look, I saw my mother go through this and it was not pretty. I always said I never wanted to marry a man like my father, but how did I miss this part. Was I to focus on the "being independent part" because I noticed she depended on him for *everything* and I never wanted to be in a relationship where I felt like I "needed a man." I purchased my own home, I had my own car and a good job, so financially I was stable! The only thing missing in my life was companionship.

Looking back, I guess I was too focused on being independent that I overlooked or forgot about my dad's cheating ways! Nevertheless, I'm asking myself, "What in the world is going on?" We've been down this road before. No, this is not the first time! Yes, I forgave him, and yes, he looked me in my eyes and promised never to do it again! After all, he was my husband, right! We did say "for better or for worst," correct?!

When he got home "late that night," it was like, he knew that I knew. He had that puppy-dog look on his face. No need for beating around the bush, so I asked, "Who is _____?" His famous words: "Oh, she's just a friend." I was calm, I wasn't irate at all, but I asked again because believe you me, I did not want to hear "She was just a friend" *again*! I gave him that look that a parent gives children that have the cookie crumbs around their mouth but said they didn't touch the cookies . . . Yeah, that one! And when he said, "She's just . . .," I stopped him!

Then I asked, "Why are you texting your friend talking about what you were or wanted to do to her?" Now we have amnesia! He doesn't know what I'm talking about. He denied the text and conversation with this young man ever took place. I started reading the text messages to him, which he allegedly sent. "That wasn't me," he replied. Then I asked, "So how did he know you had choir rehearsal today?" "I don't know, maybe he's making it up." I'm like, dude, really; this is a screen print of your phone number and signature. "How do I know he didn't just type that?" he replied. So now I'm like really irritated! I asked him to call her up and put her on speaker. She denied there being anything between them. Let me pause and say this: Most of the text messages that he sent me were exchanged between him and Mr. Not the woman; however, the context in the text messages between Mr. and the woman led up to the conversation between Mr. and the husband's text messages, got it? Okay!

Since he was still in denial, I decided to call the young man back and put him on speaker. See, it's funny how you claim you never talked to him, but now the two of you are exchanging words and you say, "I told you I'll F.U. up." Oh, wait a minute . . . how do you F_ up someone you never talked to? Okay, I'll wait _____ Yeah, still waiting, that's what I thought!

"Let me see your phone" was my next question, and of course, he deleted all his text messages, so I up one on him and went to his Facebook messages, and guess what I found? Yep, "what I was looking for?" So I started reading them out loud. Mind you, these are messages to different women. (Nothing changed.) When he realized I was in his Facebook messages, he snatched his phone out of my hand so fast, and a few choice words followed. Go figure! I had to get out of the house; I couldn't stay in the house for another minute. I don't know how long I was gone, but I doubt it was more than an hour; besides, it was late at night. But when I got in, I said my prayers and prepared for bed.

Now you think he would leave well enough alone, but no! He's still texting her at 2:00 in the morning telling her, "My wife has your husband's phone number." Dummy, the husband still had the phone and sent me the text message!

The next morning when I got up and prepared to go to church, I said to him, "It's obvious that you don't love or respect me, or even this marriage, so if you don't want to be here, leave, because I don't want anyone being with me who doesn't want me," and that was all I had to say concerning it. When I came home from church, he had already cooked dinner and was getting ready to watch the Superbowl game. I couldn't deal, and my appetite went out the window, so I went to my room and stayed there.

A few days later I called and talked to my pastor about what had happened, and he asked me to not put him out (I didn't . . . but again, I did say, "*If* you don't want to be here, leave"). He said he wanted to meet with him and talk about what was going on to see if we could work on our marriage, so I said okay! (Here I am, still willing to make it work.) When he got home, I told him what the bishop said. Two days later I came home to find him packing up all his belongings and he was gone. I was in shock because after all of that, I still wanted to work on my marriage because that's how much I loved my husband. When he closed that door behind him, I broke, I mean I broke down and I cried for only God knows how long. My fear was now my reality. Sad to say he never fought for us; he never made me feel like I was worth the fight. I was the only one fighting for our marriage. But it's like my niece said, "It's hard to fight when you're the only one in the ring!" A relationship is about give-and-take, but it seemed like I was the only one giving, and he was doing all the taking.

Oh, but he did leave a note behind and it read as follows:

"On a personal note: I want to say that you are a wonderful woman and a great wife. I want to apologize for everything that was said or done that hurt you in any way on any level. I pray that you will forgive me. I have already asked God to forgive me.

"On a business note: I will not leave you hanging financially. We have accumulated a considerable amount of debt and will not allow you to be solely responsible for it. I should be starting the new position Friday. I recommend selling the red car at CarMax. You should be able to get more than you owe. I plan to help you get caught up with the mortgage, lights, and the silver car. I know that credit card bill must be paid down also. Believe it or not, this is not the outcome I had in mind. I hope we can work together to resolve these affairs. Let me know if this is agreeable to you."

Now, ask me how much did I receive since he left? Go ahead, ask! *Not one penny!* From that day until now! He put in the divorce decree that he owed me nothing, so

I asked him about it. "You don't think you owe me anything?" So now he's saying, "Just write down what you think I owe you." Oh, so now we have amnesia! At this point, I'm like, "You know what, you owe me *nothing*!" I don't want anything from him. I'm good!

In my opinion, it was just not my ex-husband's indiscretion that ended our marriage. I believe his indiscretions were because he never wanted to be married to me. Sounds like an oxymoron, I know, but I think he wanted what I had to offer, what I represented as a godly woman. I recall during an argument him referring to leaving me as if he never wanted to be there, and when I asked what he meant by it, he didn't have a reply! As time went by, it seemed like all I had was his physical body; his heart and mind were somewhere or with someone else. He said he loved me more than I can count, but those were just words, and you can make your mouth say anything you want; besides, it takes more than love to make a relationship work! Love may take you to the altar, but love alone won't keep you in the marriage!

CHAPTER 12

TALK TO ME

I had to know what it was that caused my husband to walk away from our marriage. I couldn't just accept the fact that it was over, but why! (I heard someone ask, why do woman always need closure because *we do*, okay!) One day I called him up and invited him over to talk. I know our marriage wasn't perfect, but I thought we had something special. When he came over, we sat down, and we talked. I asked him, "What happened? Why did you leave? I thought you said God told you that I was your wife! If that's the case, why are we not together?" Cricket, cricket, cricket. (And I'm not talking about the phone company.) Nothing. He had absolutely nothing to say!

I couldn't let him get away that easily, so I asked again, and I told him, "You owe me an explanation, and I want to know why." Therefore, he proceeded to tell me that he was not connected to me sexually." I didn't have any understanding, so I ask him to explain it a little more in depth. He then said, "It wasn't that the sex wasn't good; and it wasn't the act, or positions of it, but rather the connection of the souls"! So I'm looking confused. "He was emotionally disconnected." I'm thinking, isn't your soul a combination of your mind, will, and emotions! Okay, let's see.

Mind: intellect or ability to think.
Will: to make choices or motivation
Emotion: how you feel, or passion

Okay, let me break this down. My interpretation: he's saying he was mentally and emotionally disconnected from me. In addition, he made a choice not to talk to me and express to me how he was feeling or thinking. Interesting!

Although we were married, to him our souls were not *tied*. I personally thought that was strange because don't "soul tie" spiritually when you get intimate with someone? He stated he prayed that God would bless our bed. That was the one thing he asked for because everything else was in place. (Confused.) He knew that he loved me and wanted to spend the rest of his life with me. The only thing missing was intimacy. Now, I said "confused" because he said he loved me, making love was wonderful, yet he didn't connect with me! Hmm.

Let me pause and say this. At that moment the devil tried to make me feel like waiting to be intimate was not a good idea. "If this isn't one of the biggest tricks of the enemy, I don't know what is."

You can pray all you want for something, but if you're not willing to deal with the demons in your past or your secret sins, then total deliverance will not take place.

The problem here is, he was praying for the gratification of his flesh, but not for deliverance for his soul. See, you just can't stop at asking God for a good sex life. You also need to pray and ask God to deliver you from your past sins and to help you overcome the lust of your flesh. You need to call some things out by name and cast them out, especially if you know you're a whoremonger or carry the seed of your father!

"No one sews a patch of unshruken cloth on an old garment. Otherwise, the new piece will pull away from the old making the tear worse. And no one pours new wine into old wineskins. Otherwise, the wine will burst the skins, and the wineskins will be ruined. No, they pour new wine into new wineskins" (Mark 2: 21, 22). NIV

As he was talking, the Lord revealed something to me in the spirit, so I said to him, "Is it possible that you couldn't 'connect' with me because you never let go of the other billion women you slept with in your past? Is it possible that you're still tied to them and that's one of the reasons you couldn't connect with me?" He sat there with that dumb look on his face like, "Hey, I never thought about that," then he shrugged his shoulders like, oh well.

Any marriage is worth fighting for if both parties are willing to put in the work, but my ex-husband didn't leave the marriage when he walked out. He left way before I even realized he was gone. So again, as the scripture states, *You cannot pour new wine into old wineskins.* Likewise, you cannot build a new marriage holding on to your lustful past and the women in it. I'm not saying he didn't love me, but there are some things you just must let go of in order for the marriage to work! I honestly believed we could've had a beautiful marriage, but in my opinion, he never let go of his past.

When I talked to his mother about what happened, she was shocked, but not too surprising. She said, "I thought he would be different because he saw what I went through with his father. He was the same way, and he knew how I felt about it!" She kept apologizing for what he did, and I had to explain to her that it was not her fault. She raised him the best she knew how. He knew right from wrong; he chose to do wrong, therefore that was on him.

Looking back, it made me question everything I thought I believed. Now it sounds like the devil is talking to me like he did Eve in Genesis: "Hath God said"! At this point, I really don't know! Now I'm thinking about what I said in chapter 9! Was it just me? I'm second-guessing everything I once believed. Did God not speak? Did I make it all up in my head, and was I living in denial?

One day, leaving the grocery store, I sent him a text. I said to him, "You told me God said I was your wife; now either you're lying, or God is lying." He responded, "That is what I said. God did tell me that!" Now my confusion is at another level because how can you say God told you that I was your wife, but you still walked away! So, what you're saying is you're not a liar, but you made a choice to override what you claimed God said to you? Oh, okay, wow! Well, someone is lying but it's not God, I'm just saying! Let me say this for the record: I loved my husband until the ink dried on our divorced papers, and I refused to let anyone make me feel guilty for it! Period!

It's important to pray, but it's also important to pray in *secret* (in tongues). We sometimes don't understand how important that is. Paul said, "*I pray in the Spirit and I pray with an understanding.*" When you pray in your strength, you're telling God your plans and desires, but when you pray in the Spirit, you're allowing God to use you to pray his plan and desires.

"Likewise the Spirit helps our infirmities for we know not what we should pray as we ought, but the Spirit himself makes intercession for us with groaning which cannot understand" (Rom. 8:26). KJV

CHAPTER 13

LETTERS TO MR.

LETTER # 1

"Through thick and thin I was there for you! I had your back when your back was against the wall. When you lost your job and no money was coming in, I supported you! I never talked down at you and never once belittled you. I've never made you feel less than a man. Through all the hardship I was there for you! You faced a lot of roadblocks, but I encouraged you and I supported you, and never once did I turn my back on you! I was always true to you. I prayed for you and I loved you with everything within me despite all we went through! You were the one unfaithful in this marriage and that had nothing to do with me! I kept my part of the 'better or for worst,' but when it got worst for me, you left! You left me by myself and with all these bills! So here I stand with no husband, no job, and no income! That was a cowardly move! I hope to God that you don't treat the next woman the way you treated me, and I pray to God that she doesn't treat you the way you treated me! Because that's the only way you'll ever know how you really hurt me! So, thanks for, as you put, it 'not wanting to hurt me'!"

Looking back, I know for a fact my ex-husband never fought for me. He never fought for us! Even though he was the one in the wrong, I was the one fighting for our marriage. I was the one fighting and pleading for him to come home because I still wanted our marriage to work. But the saying is true: "How can you fight when there's only one person in the ring?" He took his off the moment he left me. Even at our divorce hearing, it seemed like he couldn't wait for it to be over so he can go and officially start his new life with his new lover. And no, I did not put up a fight; I gave him what he wanted. My thing was this, call me crazy if you want, but I was willing to fight until the end. But once those papers were signed, the gloves came off! I was done!"

LETTER # 2

"Just thinking so I thought I would share. I don't know what your plans are if you're trying to find yourself, find someone else, or just playing the field! Nevertheless, I pray for you every day. I pray and ask God to guide your heart and thoughts, among other things. I don't know if you want to work on getting back together or if you already filed for divorce. But I would ask this of you: Pray! Set aside a time to pray and ask God if you should work on this marriage or if you should walk away! If he says work on it, then you should come home, but if he says walk away, then let me know and I will leave you alone and never bother you again! But you must be honest with God, yourself, and with me! Now if you don't pray, then that would mean one of two things. One, you don't care, or two, you're afraid to find out the truth! So again, if you want me to leave you alone, pray, seek God's face for the answer (I think you owe me that much), and if he says walk away, then I *promise* you, that's exactly what I will do too! You can get the papers and I will sign them with no hesitation! It would be freedom for you and closure for me!"

Again, I got no response.

"But he that is married careth for the things that are of the world, how he may please his wife" (1 Cor. 7:33, KJV).

"Husbands, love your wives, even as Christ also loved the church, and gave himself for it; That he might sanctify and cleanse it with the washing of water by the word, That he might present it to himself a glorious church, not having spot, or wrinkle, or any such thing; but that it should be holy and without blemish. So ought men to love their wives as their own bodies. He that loveth his wife loveth himself. For no man ever yet hated his own flesh; but nourisheth and cherisheth it, even as the Lord the church: For we are members of his body, of his flesh, and of his bones. For this, the cause shall a man leave his father and mother and shall be joined unto his wife, and they two shall be one flesh" (Eph. 5:25–31, KJV).

Letter #3 was a prayer: "Father, in Jesus's name I ask you to touch my husband! I ask you to open his eyes along with his understanding. I pray, God, that you would minister to him throughout the day and in the midnight hour! I pray that when he sleeps, you would speak to him in dreams; I also pray that you would remind him of your promises. Father, I also pray that you would keep him and protect him, mind, soul, and body! He is your child, and you created him to worship you in the spirit of holiness. God, it's no longer about me or what I want but rather what you want in his life.

"Your plan has been set from the beginning of time; help him to walk it out! I pray that you would bind the hand of the enemy and break every chain that has him in spiritual bondage! (Whom the son sets free is free indeed.) I bind every demonic spirit, every spirit of deception, corruption, every lustful demon, and every generational curse over his life! For your word states in Matthew 18:18: *Whatsoever you shall bind on earth shall be bound in heaven: and whatsoever you shall loose on earth shall be loosed in heaven. Therefore, I decree and declare the word of the Lord to be established in his life . . . that it will not return void!* Lord, use him for your glory! May you cause him to see the truth. Remove the blinders. Also Father, allow him to see who his true friends are and cut off every lying demon, and let him not be blind to the devil's plan. And because I'm reminded that you're God, I know that you will get the glory out of this! This I pray in Jesus's name. Amen!"

Letter # 4: "I miss you so much it hurts! My heart feels like it's broken in a million pieces. I miss the times we spent laughing at the craziest things! The way you would look at me when you didn't believe what someone was saying. It was our inside joke! The way we fell to sleep with our legs wrapped around each other . . . crazy, but that was our thing. Or the way I would inspect your body even though you would accuse me of not doing it! The way you looked at me from across the room or grab me after church because you were hungry and I wasn't moving fast enough! I just miss us, that's all!"

I never got a response back from any of the letters or prayer I sent. I wondered if he just deleted them, because he didn't want to read them, or maybe he read them and just didn't care. Well, I'll never know and at this point in my life, I'm good with that.

Some might say, well, you prayed, but God didn't answer your prayer! Well, you're partially right. The beautiful thing about prayer and human is this: God is not going to override someone's decision. Understanding that person's spirit must agree with your prayer. He made the decision not to! In addition, as stated we pray in the Spirit and we pray with an understanding. The prayer that was prayed in the spirit was answered according to the will of God! Besides, he could have also been praying to God about something totally different!

CHAPTER 14

THINKING OUT LOUD
. . . MY THOUGHTS

If I only gave him "some" of me, it would have been easier for me to let go, as he did with me, but I was all in! My love was real, and it was genuine. I really thought we would be together until death parted us. In retrospect, it did, because divorce is like death, depending on what side of the table you on! I told myself I don't ever want to love someone again to where I lose myself in the process.

Now I'm thinking the demons in my closet have come out to taunt me! Maybe, just maybe, if I shared with him the secrets of my past, things might have been different. Who knew there was a possibility that it could affect my marriage? Besides, it didn't happen to him; it happened to me. Is it possible that my being molested or raped caused our souls not to tie since he felt no connection; could it really be my fault that my marriage ended because I didn't enlighten him? I mean, was it really that important! It's not something I talked about. As a matter of fact, I never talked about it. Well, I talked to God about it so that should have been okay, right? Besides, I was intimate in other relationships and it didn't affect them, so why would it affect him? Nevertheless, here I am thinking about it. I'm still trying to figure out what went wrong. Maybe I think too much! But I have no understanding as to why he did what he did. But the reality of it is, he did what he did because it was in him to do. It's called choices: We all have the ability to choose!

The enemy would like for me to feel guilty, but regardless of what I did or didn't do, said or didn't say, were never grounds for adultery, period!

To love with forgiveness, you must take on the mind of Christ because the enemy brings back to your remembrances all the hurt and pain that was caused by the person. To let go is so much easier. Yes, you can move on to someone else, but the person is still there.

For example, do you ever wonder why some women that have children—I said "some"—are now in other relationships or even married but still give the fathers of their child(ren) a hard time? Now you can disagree with me if you want to, but think about it for a second! They moved on, but they didn't let go! Why, because if they really did, there would be some common ground between the both of them. If that man is paying child support and going out of his way to be there for his child(ren), why wouldn't she let him be there for his child(ren)? Why is there an issue with who he's dating? Why is it a problem for that child(ren) to spend the weekend with "their father" if he's doing what he's supposed to as a man!

Because somewhere deep down, she never let go of the love, pain, or *him*! And vice versa! One of the things that get me is some women are quick to tell their child's father, "Don't have my baby around no other woman," but have his child around another man! If that's not a double standard, I don't know what is! Please *stop it*! Don't let denial be your permanent residence. Let go of that bitterness and unforgiveness and be free to really love again.

Nevertheless, it was not that easy for me, to say the least, but it did happen over time through much prayer and fasting. Lord knows I had to stay in prayer because every time I heard his name, I wanted to punch him in the face or run him over with my car, but hey, I'm not a violent person, just thoughts that entered my mind, but for real, I did want to punch him in the face but had to remind myself that's an assault and I could go to jail. That's one of the reasons I try my best to keep my hands off people. But hear me though, this thing about matters of the heart will cause you to hurt someone in the worst way (I've seen it) if you lead with your emotions. That's why we have to get ourselves together! Never let anyone push you to the point of no return to where you lose yourself because they are no longer a part of your life. They are not worth you going to jail or losing your life or freedom. It might take time, but you can get over it and you can love again.

OH, MY BROTHER

It would hurt me to my heart when I heard brothers talking about how much they love their wives when I was going through my divorce, and to see how they treat their family with so much love and respect was taunting me. You have brothers in the world loving and being faithful to their spouses and some brothers in the church who claim (pretend) and act like they love God but don't know what it means to be faithful.

I'm not saying all the men in the world are faithful, nor am I saying that all of the brothers in the church are unfaithful. But it does raise an eyebrow when you take into account the divorce rate in churches these days, especially when the men of God should be setting the standard and leading by example for the world to follow. Sadly, they are trailing behind like lost puppies with their tail between their legs.

Questions for the men:

Are you training your sons to be men, husbands, and fathers?
Are you training them to be like you, good or bad?
Would you let your daughters date a man like you?
What are you putting in them considering they are the next generation?

Oh, how I wish that men would rise and take their rightful place in the kingdom, and to know the will of God for their lives. Not just quote scriptures that are popular but searching the scriptures and allow the Holy Spirit to minister to them from the depths of their souls, teaching them how to be God-fearing men. Stop allowing pride to override what you should be doing according to God's word, and not what you think is popular according to the world's standards.

I want you to be free from the concerns of this life. An unmarried man can spend his time doing the Lord's work and thinking about how to please him (1 Cor. 7:32, NLT).

CHAPTER 15

WHAT ABOUT ME

Was I the perfect wife? Yes, of course, I was! Just kidding. (I had to laugh at that one.) I was far from it. I got on his nerves, I'm sure, but that's a part of merging two lives together. Sometimes I would speak my mind, and sometimes I held my peace! That was hard sometimes because I know how this mouth of mine works. It was hard to hold back once you popped the top! Regina used to say, "I had to have the last word," but I looked at it as I had to get my point across! I know she'll be reading this saying, "No, chick, you had to have the last word!" (She's right, she's right, she's right, in my bishop's voice!) Tell the truth and shame the devil, but she did too, so oh well. However, I'm in a better place now!

Although I was supportive of his music, I didn't care to go with him to his venues in the beginning. That's because some of the places he went I didn't care to go, so I had to put self to the side. I felt if he wasn't going anywhere that would cause me harm or nightclubs, I went and supported him.

Our house wasn't dirty, but sometimes I didn't feel like cleaning or doing my hair! (Don't look at me crazy.) I worked two jobs and when I got home from my second job (on my feet from doing other people's hair all night), I would be tired. However, I wasn't the only one living in the house, and he was home more than I was. Besides marriage is give-and-take. We both had to work together.

I fault myself because some of the things I should have spoken up about I didn't. We tend to have this could-should-would mentality. Like I should have said, "I hate your eggs," among other things, but I didn't! Or hey, "You do know I can cook too, right?" But again, I didn't! Let him tell it. He was the only one that knew his way around the kitchen, and guess what, since he liked doing it, I let him! There was a lot I could have said, but I didn't! See, the victim tends to blame themselves for things they have no control over. I could have been the perfect wife, doing everything he wanted me to! Cooking, cleaning, sexing, talking, dancing, grooming, working, or whatever, he still would not have been satisfied. Funny because "I wish there was a day where I didn't had to ask him to go cut the grass, and end up doing it myself because I waited over a week for it to get done," but I'm going to stay on how much of a good wife I wasn't! Oh, but wait . . . He never said I wasn't a good wife; he said our "souls didn't tie"!

See, the problem here, in my opinion, was he was never satisfied. How does one commit adultery and cheat on the adulteress? Yes, we were still legally married, but he was living with his girlfriend, yet blowing up my phone wanting to get it in. At first, I was like, "Boy, bye," but I was reminded that legally, that body still belonged to me! So, um yeah, I opened the cookie jar once, twice, three times maybe. But then it hit me, this is not going to work in my favor because he's playing her the same way he played me. "How is it that you're all in love with her but blowing up my phone!" Yeah, no . . . even had the nerve to ask if we could do it one last time before finalizing the divorce. I couldn't do it anymore, even though we were still legally married. I know my worth, and I know I deserve better! So, you see, that foolishness about our "souls not tying" was, in my opinion, an excuse for him to leave! Water is sweeter when stolen!

Since I don't like to assume, I don't have a problem asking questions, so I asked him of his preference like when it came to the bedroom! You know, I was like, "So hey, what do you like, or don't like? Are you into roleplay? What's your fantasy?" I wanted to know what I as a wife needed to do to please my husband. Me personally, I wanted to experience roleplay. You know like "the landlord and the tenant," that part where "someone forgot to pay their rent; so what are we going to do about it"! This is something I expressed to him. And if I suggested something, it appears to go in one ear and out the other.

Every romantic gesture was on me! And if I tried to tell him something, I was shut down. Like one night I said to him, "Why don't you try this?" and his reply was, "Who's doing this, me or you?" So let me do it! But I'm thinking, yeah, but you're not doing it right! (I know I should have said it, but I didn't.) He made me feel like I was challenging his manhood. But this isn't the fifties where women just lay there and let their husbands do whatever they want to them! We're a team; we're supposed to talk about this.

Nevertheless, I left it alone and didn't say anything else after that, but I would try and hint from time to time. Sometimes he got it, but most of the time he didn't or just didn't care. However, nothing I did screamed "go cheat on me" because despite all we've been through, I was there for him. I put my feelings to the side and tried to be the wife he needed me to be even if I wasn't the wife he wanted me to be!

After waiting fifteen years to be with my husband, I had some tricks up my sleeves. Unfortunately, over 65 percent of them are still there! See, I always know there was a freak in me, but I didn't know to what extent until I separated from him.

One night I got a call from my sister wanting me to download Skype on my phone so that I could video chat with my dad as he was in the hospital and the doctors didn't know if he was going to make it overnight. Nonetheless, Skype was too large so she advised me to download another video chat program (no, I'm naming it) new to me, so I did and in the process of doing so, it asked me to add a picture. I thought nothing of it, so I did thinking it was for my sisters. Suddenly, I started getting likes and comments on my picture popping up and I thought, "Who are these people liking my picture?" On the other hand, when I opened the program, I noticed there were men all over the world. And yes, I started chatting with some of them.

There was this one guy. Let's call him "Jerome." He was very sweet and thoughtful. We chatted for a few weeks. About a month or so into it, he asked to video chat. At first, I was reluctant because I didn't know much about him, but his argument was we live in two different states. He said, "I might not ever get a chance to see you in person," and I thought, "Hey, he's right!" I told him I would think about it, and a week later we started video chatting. It's crazy how in that short amount of time he woke up a part of me that I thought was dead. He spoke to the woman in me that was broken, mistreated, and abandoned—the woman who said she would never love again or get married because her ex made her feel like no man would want to be with her if they knew why he left.

No man would want to wait until marriage because as, he put it, "the sex was great, but there was no connection." I still don't get it, but anyway, she didn't want to hear that again. It's sad to say, but he woke up something in me that Mr. was never able to do for the five years we were married! As I listened to him talk, I found myself in a tug-of-war, because I'm now intrigued with what he had to say! My flesh is saying, "This man knows what he's talking about. Tell me more!" but my spirit was saying, "Girl, you know God is watching you," and I'm saying, "Lord, have mercy" because he was able to tap into me with just his words! And the things he said, I need a fan just thinking about it! I felt like Paul in Galatians 5:17: "For the flesh lusts against the Spirit and the Spirit against the flesh and these are contrary to one another, that you may not do the things that you desire."

He said, "Talk to me! Tell me your fantasy!" and I was like, "Um . . . hmm . . . well, maybe, but no, I can't do that!" But he didn't have a problem sharing his with me. As he talked, I listened, and as I listened, I craved his words even more. Listening to him was like watching a movie because I saw everything he said. Crazy as it sounds, I felt validated, and I felt wanted, like someone finally noticed me. It was like he saw what I wanted Mr. to see, but never took notice of! He explored my body mentally. I didn't realize how much of me wanted him until he tapped into me, and I thought, *Wait a minute!* Sin is a powerful beast! Here I am entertaining a man I don't even know and was enjoying it. As he talked, I envisioned the police knocking on the door saying, "Ma'am, you're in violation of LOA. I'm going to have to arrest you . . ."

"But Officer, what's LOA?"

"Lack of Affection, ma'am!"

"I'm guilty as charged, Officer! I guess you're going to have to arrest me!"

Yes, I would go into fantasy mood just like that.

Don't get it twisted, I was still aware of what was going on. I was not that far gone. I acknowledge the struggle that was going on between my flesh and my spirit! At one point I said, "Jesus, close your eyes" because I needed his attention, but in the midst of all that, I still had mixed emotions. I was angry, bitter, sad, happy, confused, laughing, and crying! Because again, here I am entertaining a man who was saying everything I wanted and needed from my ex, but he was too busy giving it to someone else! I wanted to escape. I wanted to let go of my inhibition and be free to do whatever I "felt" with no strings holding me back. I was a good girl for far too long. Seems like good girls never win anyway, so why not be bad for a change. My flesh was saying, "Do it, do it!" but the truth is, I couldn't do it! I wanted to so badly, but I just couldn't! Not just with him, but with any man. I sat on my bed and screamed, "Lord, why!" Needless to say, I had to stop calling him because again, I found myself in a tug-of-war. It was flesh versus spirit, and my flesh was wild awake and up to the challenge!

"So now it is no longer I who do it, but sin that dwells within me. For I know that nothing good dwells in me, that is in my flesh. For I have the desire to do what is

right, but not the ability to carry it out. For I do not do the good I want, but the evil I do not want is what I keep on doing" (Rom. 7:17–19, ESV).

I've been in this walk a long time, so yielding to my flesh was not as easy as I thought it would be. My prayer has always been, "Lord, keep me." And at that moment where I needed him the most, he showed up and reminded me of what I asked him to do! Nevertheless, the struggle was still real! And to be honest, I was mad with God. I couldn't understand why he would allow my marriage to end and cause my flesh to go through such traumatic stress. It was like coming off a seven-day fast and you sit down to a nice juicy steak with loaded baked potato for dinner (or your favorite meal) and someone accidentally knocks it off the table and steps on it. That's the closest I can get to describing how I felt! And yet I still must trust that God is too wise to make a mistake!

CHAPTER 16

LET GO AND LET GOD

When it comes to forgiveness, it's not just about forgiving the person or people that hurt you, but it's also about forgiving yourself. One of the reasons you must forgive yourself is because you don't want to hold yourself as a prisoner to the crime that was committed against you. You don't only forgive people for them, but you also do it to set "yourself" free!

EXERCISE TIME

Get a mirror or stand in the mirror and repeat these words (or whatever the Lord puts in your heart.) We'll just call my words a diving board to get you started.

I am fearfully and wonderfully made.
I can do all things through Christ that strengthens me.
No weapon formed against me shall prosper
What the enemy meant for my bad is working in my favor.
I am *more* than a conqueror through Christ Jesus.
No matter what the enemy throws my way, God has given me gloves to catch it.
I'm not what the worlds say I am. I am who God created me to be.

This is only a test! (I want my *A*.)

I am no longer afraid of:

_____

_____

I will no longer be bound by:

_____

_____

My past is just that. The past and my future will be better because:

_____

_____

Sometimes when I look in the mirror, I see myself as:

_____

_____

But other times I see myself as:

_____

_____

I used to think that I would never get over this:

_____

_____

The pain that was caused by _____ will not keep me in bondage because:

_____

_____

I am standing on God's word and will look at this as a test that was designed to take me to the next level. The devil thought he could stop me, but look at me now. I am:

_____

_____

_____

LET US PRAY

Dear Heavenly Father, forgive me for blaming myself for the things I took to heart that was out of my control. I thought that I was powerless, and I didn't know I had the power within me to speak life over my situation. I stand in repentance, and I declare that I am not a victim, but a victor! I stand stronger, wiser, and better and it's all because of you, Lord. I can indeed do all things and I know that you will continue to strengthen me. Thank you for loving me beyond me and showing me how to love myself. Amen!

Now that you have forgiven yourself, it's time to forgive the ones who wronged you! We are not going backward but moving forward to a bigger and brighter future. Amen!

Let me say this: Everyone's situation is different, so don't think because you didn't go through what another brother or sister went through that your test was small or not important! (Remember, God's word said he won't put any more on you than *you* can bear!) Your trail is your trail and you have every right to be affected by it! Healing is a process, so while you're in the process, go through it so that God can get the glory! When God has delivered you and healed you in an area, strengthen your brother or sister. Allow your test to be a testimony to help heal and deliver someone else. God knows who needs it and he will allow them to cross your path when the time is right.

CHAPTER 17

THINKING OUT LOUD

One of the things that bothered me during my separation from my husband was some of the comments I got from people. I can count on one hand how many people were supportive and had my back. Some of the words out of their mouths were:

"God got someone better for you."
"His loss."
"Don't worry about it. You'll be all right."
And my favorite: "You were more spiritual than him anyway!"

Oh really! If that's the case, what do you say to the pastor that divorced his wife? How spiritual was he? I won't be holding my breath for an answer on this one, so let's move on!

Meanwhile, I'm looking like wow! Really! So, you mean to tell me that the same God you say have the heart of the king in his hands can't touch the heart of my husband. The same God who said he ordains marriage can't put mine back together. The same God that says, "I know the thoughts I think toward you, says the Lord, thoughts of peace and not of evil, to bring you to an expected end," can't restore us back as one!

Wait, wait, wait . . .
The same God who said, "I will not cut short your expectation."
The God who said, "Whatsoever you desire when you pray to believe"!

That same God can't deliver my husband and bring him back to me, is what you're saying?

My faith was so strong that I knew he and I would get back together, and I was like, "Come on, devil, you want to fight? Let's fight!" I prayed, I fasted, I consecrated, I had personal shut-ins, I got in the prayer lines, I planted seeds (offerings), I cried out at the altar. At times I would record my prayers and when I didn't have the strength to pray, I would hit the Play button and listen to my prayers! (By the way, that's a good idea; you should try it.) The enemy started talking to me: "You're going to be single again. I thought it was going to last forever." "It's too late for you to have children." "You're going to die alone!" Oh, he was working overtime in my mind!

Yes, I entertained those thoughts for a minute so there was no "casting down of imaginations"! I really felt like giving up! Notice I said "felt" the thing with feelings as they change, so never trust them. I did everything I thought I knew to do, and I knew God was going to turn this around for me. After all, I'm an intercessor! I know how to get a prayer through, right!

Well, the fact of the matter is, God can do anything he wants to do, when he wants to, and how he wants to! My question was why he's not doing it for me. Well, God gives man free will, and God is not going to override his decision by force because that would go against God's nature! It's like salvation—he presents it to you, but you have a choice to accept or deny him. I started to feel alone and abandoned. I felt like God really did forsake me. It got to the point where I felt nothing, I saw nothing, and I heard nothing! It felt like God had left the building. His presence was nowhere to be found. It was just me, myself, and I! I was all I had! No angels showed up to minister to me during prayer. No dreams to let me know everything was going to be okay! I was in a spiritual wilderness; it was a very dry and dark place in my life. I honestly didn't know what I was going to do.

What amazed me was how God continued to use me in ministry; it was like I didn't miss a beat. Intercessory prayer, on it! Altar workers ministry, did it? Prison ministry, you couldn't stop me from doing it! Looking back now, I understand why he allowed me to continue to minister. I believe he knew those ministries served as the fuel that kept me going! Had I not stayed active in church, I might have self-destructed! Actually, he was there all along, being the omnipotent one, but to me, it felt like he wasn't where I needed him to be.

After our separation, my ex-husband made me feel like everything I did was wrong. For 2.5 seconds, I felt like there was no need to wait until marriage anymore to be intimate with a man. Heck, now I'm feeling like, "Go test the waters if you will. Everyone else doing it, and enjoying it. No condemnation on their part, so why not join the crowd!" Oh, but I've never been one to follow the crowd; I don't fit in, I stand out! See, I know that was just a trick of the enemy, so I didn't entertain that thought for long!

Months went by. No calls, no text. *Nothing*! When he left, he took everything he owned, including my self-esteem. As I watched him leave from the back room, I hit the floor in tears; I don't think I have ever experienced such pain in my life.

It felt like someone literally put their hand into my chest, ripped out my heart, took a nail gun and started shooting into it, then put it in the fire and burned it until it was like charcoal, then turned around and put it in the freezer until it was cold as ice. And if that wasn't bad enough, they took it outside and smashed it on the concrete (with the nails still in it) as it broke into countless pieces, only for the sun to come along and cause it to melt while I stood by and watched as it went down the drain. That's the gist of it.

I prayed and I cried. I cried and I prayed! Truth be told, I practically cried myself to sleep just about every night wondering what I did wrong, and what could I have done to make him love me. (*We can't make anyone love us, period.*) Sometimes when you truly love someone, the hardest thing to do is walk away. You tend to hold on to the person even though they did you wrong. Sometimes I wonder if it's the pain they caused or the embarrassment of what people would say . . . could be a little of both, but my heart was very heavy!

Yeah, I know people talked about me because it always got back to me. Truth be told, there was a like sting, but after it faded, I could care less about what people had to say since I knew I did the right thing.

"My soul thirsteth for God, for the living God: when shall I come and appear before God? My tears have been my meat day and night, while they continually say unto me, where is thy God?" (Ps. 42:2, 3).

Trust me, I wanted to know where he was too because it felt like he was nowhere to be found! I've been in love before, but I have never experienced this level of pain and betrayal. With all that I was going through and all that I've been through, I had to ask God, "Was I created just for trials and tribulations?" because it seemed like my whole life was trying! I was always going through something. If it wasn't one thing, it was another. (You too, I know I'm not alone.)

What's funny to me (*not laughing*) is when some of the men in the church divorce their wives and they'll get married in the same year, and no one talks about it or him. He gets a pat on the back and congratulations, yet the same people expect a woman to wait forever. They're like, "Girl, you need to wait on God!" Well, my question is, "Who did he wait on?"

They have the nerve to try and use scripture to back up their actions talking about "it's not good for man to be alone," but when it comes to the women, they want to quote 1 Corinthians 7:9, talking about "But if they cannot contain, let them marry, for it is better to marry than to burn." What! First, why do we have to be the ones burning? If you ask me, it looks like they're the ones on fire, or better yet, can't control their flesh. Look, I'm not saying all, I'm just saying!

We are living in a day where tomorrow (heck, today) is not promising. I'm not telling you to go out and just marry anyone, but what I am saying is you better live your life and stop worrying about what people think or what they have to say because at the end of the day, it's your life and it should be pleasing to God and not man. Besides, long as you got God's approval, man's approval doesn't matter. Oh, but please don't make any hasty decisions, and make sure that it's really God!

Oh, but here's the flip side of that, are we waiting on God or is he waiting on us? If the saying is true that God has already put everything inside of us that we need, and he has set everything in motion since the beginning of time, then it's up to us to seek God's face for truth and direction concerning every area of our lives. It's a matter of us growing into and perfecting what his plan and purpose are for our lives. Do you agree or disagree? _____ Oh my! Nevertheless, make every decision a prayerful decision, and make sure it's God and not the voices in your head telling you yes! Go in your prayer closet and have a little take with Jesus!

"For the Lord God is a sun and shield: the Lord will give grace and glory: no good thing will he withhold from them that walk uprightly" (Ps. 84:11, AKJ).

CHAPTER 18

GET BACK UP

After my marriage failed, I wanted to go out and sin on purpose, as in fornicate, get busy, do the wild thing! Yep, I said it! To me, it seemed like most of the people I knew that was "sinning" seemed to be getting blessed.

Case in point: One couple that was fornicating got married, another couple who fornicated got pregnant, then they got married, and another got pregnant, miscarried, then got married, and seem to be living happily ever after.

So, now I'm looking back, trying to figure out where I went wrong. Is there some truth to the "test-drive theory"? After all, everyone is living in marital bliss and my marriage is going down the drain! So now I'm thinking I'll have to experiment with the next one! But that devil is still a liar! I had to remind myself that regardless of what it "looks like," God's way is still and always will be right. (*Oh, for the record, those relationships didn't last either.*)

Don't believe the hype; God's way is always right even when things didn't or don't go as planned. People will try to make you feel like you made a mistake with that "I told you so" look on their face (rolling my eyes), but it is the enemy's job to make you feel as if God is not on your side, but he is still a liar! We may not always understand why God allows some of the things that happen in our lives, but Romans 8:28 reminds us that it's all working together for our good!

A pastor friend said something that stuck with me, and that is, "The end of a caterpillar is the beginning of a beautiful butterfly." So you might be crawling along right now, but keep moving, and when you reach that place where you can go no farther, rest in God. Before you know it, he will give you wings to fly, and when he does, spread your wings and be free!

Sometimes, I hear people say (well, I said it too), "Tell the truth; shame the devil." "I want everything the devil stole" because they think that everything I lost was taken by the devil. But the truth of the matter is, there are some things the devil stole, but there are some things God removed from our lives. And we need to understand the difference, especially when it comes to our prayer!

Here's how that looks. With our mouth, we're saying, "I want everything the devil stole from us (because we think everything lost is stolen)," but in our hearts/minds, we're saying, "I want *everything* back, I want my spouse back, my home back, my job back, my car back, my friends back, my relationship (male/female) back."

The question is, "How do we know what was stolen and what was removed?" If we think about it, sometimes we don't! However, I don't want anything back that God removed. Understand that if God removed it, it was for a reason. Therefore, if something comes up missing in our lives, our prayer should be, "God, did you remove it or did the devil take it?" That way, we'll know how to target our prayer!

Some of us need a revelation of Jeremiah 18: 1–6.

The word that came to Jeremiah from the Lord: Arise, and god down to the potter's house, and there I will let you hear my words. So I went down to the potter's house, and there he was working at his wheel. And the vessel he was making of clay was spoiled in the potter's hand, and he reworked it into another vessel, as it seemed good to the potter to do. Then the word of the Lord came to me: O House of Israel, can I not do with you as this potter has done? declares the Lord, Behold, Like the clay in the potter's hand, so are you in my hand, O house of Israel. KJV

When we go down to the potter's house, we can get a better understanding of why God is doing what he's doing in our lives. Sometimes, he breaks us just to make us new again! But the beauty in it is we're in his hands.

I don't care how strong of a person you think you are. Next to death, nothing breaks or hurts a person like a person they love. Notice that I didn't say "love" hurts but rather the person that they trust or given their hearts to! When the person you love doesn't see you the way you desire them to, when the love you have is not reciprocated, when everything in you says look at me, hold me, caress me, I need you to love me, but it seems like they're looking back at you like "what do you want?," acting as if you caught them off guard or something. But on the other hand, they don't have a clue and they're sure as heaven not able to catch you in the spirit. If that's not frustrating at times, I don't know what is!

It's important to remember that God gave us free will, and sometimes people make choices beyond our control. Unfortunately there's nothing we can do about it other than pray and ask God to give us the strength to make it through the process. Stop trying to validate or make yourself feel more important to them by saying, "You'll never find another person like me." That's the point; they don't want another person like you. For example, when I met my ex, I was abstinent. He didn't want another woman that was abstinent; he wanted someone that was giving it up, and that relationship still didn't last! So, don't waste your time on dressing up in your "oh, he/she gone, wish they never left you" outfit. Just make yourself a better you for the next person that walks into your life!

A Little Poem

The moment when you realize that you did it God's way
And it seemed like everything went wrong along the way
and all you want to do was to run away!
But you stood firm, knowing that there will be a better day!
Take a deep breath . . . Inhale, now exhale
Now, you're reminded to count it all joy, because
It's working together for your good anyway
Well, thank God for helping you along the way
and take time to praise him for a brighter day

CHAPTER 19

WILL I LOVE AGAIN?

My hope and prayer are that I will love again. I can be honest and say that after my divorce, I thought that I would never want to love again, but God allowed some awesome men to come into my life and they reminded me that life was not over because of the divorce. Personally, I wasn't ready to date, but I learned a lot from them. I was reminded that my life had meaning and purpose, and that I still had a lot of love in me to give.

I remember years ago I would meet all kinds of men, but the Lord said to me, "I'm not bringing them into your life for you to date; I'm bringing them for you to minister to!" So now, here I am, many years later going through a similar situation, but this time it seemed as if they were ministering to me.

But like I was saying, I met some of the sweetest men. Some of them thought they could offer me the world, but how could they when it wasn't theirs to give? Nonetheless, they treated me with the utmost respect. Unfortunately, I was not able to give them what they might have wanted in return. (I was still broken.) Some wanted friendship, others romantic relationship/love, and some whatever they could find. But one thing is sure: I never led them on. I knew my heart was not ready for anything romantic, and I knew I had to be made whole before opening that door again. However, I was honest with my intentions from the beginning, and I made it clear that friendship was all I had to offer. Now, if they wanted to continue seeing me, it was on them and I was fine with that.

Again, there were lessons to be learned, so I had to pay attention. It was like a new birth, learning to love again, starting with me. There is no way I could give my heart to someone and don't know how to love me first. Loving me is embracing the total being. That's the good, the bad, and the ugly! If I'm not complete, then I'm expecting him to overlove me to make up for what I'm not giving myself or what I'm lacking! That would not be fair to him (I know everyone is different), but I had to look in the mirror and say, "I love you" and I want what's best for you!

I started dating "me" again. I would take myself out to breakfast, lunch, and dinner, table for one, please, and thank you! I love live bands, so I'd go pull up a chair at a local event and order a "Shirley Temple loaded with cherries." Sometimes, I'd take a drive down to St. Augustine or even to the downtown Jacksonville to listen to the live band on the weekend. Not to mention going to the beach, different parks, sightseeing at different venues, or hitting the road to Miami or somewhere in Georgia, just to name a few. I didn't sit around waiting for someone to invite me out in order to have a good time. I enjoy my own company!

See, I was feeling like the ugly duckling. After my marriage ended, I had to change the way I felt and saw myself. I had to remind myself that "I" was beautiful regardless of how anyone else saw me. Self-hate was trying to creep in, but I started seeing myself the way God intended me to.

I remember getting out of prayer one morning, and as I was leaving out of the room, I heard this song in my spirit. The melody was playing as I heard "open my eyes . . ." I tried listening for the rest of the lyrics, but they didn't come. However, the melody was still playing, so I logged on to YouTube and typed in "open my eyes"; nothing came up. I kept playing the melody in my head, trying to figure out the rest of the song, so I removed that and put in "make me believe." I don't know where that came from other than looking back, I knew it was *God*, but as I scrolled down, I saw Bishop Morton's song *"I Am What You See."* When I hit play, I was blown away. I knew God put that song by the Spirit because I don't recall listening to it. I was not just fearfully and wonderfully made, but I saw myself as attractive, beautiful, and intelligent. I was what God saw in me! I am what he sees. He sees me victorious, he sees me faithful, he sees me believing that he is more than able!

I've always conducted myself as a lady, and I know I had more to offer than just my body. Furthermore, I know what my expectations are, so I'm not going to settle for less. I'm not being picky, but I have a preference. It's not so much about height, color, or size, but more of the heart and intentions.

Some people are quick to say, "You're passing up a good man/woman," but that good person might not be the person God wanted for you to help fulfill your destiny. The two of you might be on different pages, heck, even different books in life.

You hear it all the time: "He/she is a good man/woman, but is he/she the right man/woman for you?"

I believe that if you're dating with a purpose, sex should remain off the table until you get to really know each other. Me, personally, until marriage, but that's just me. Unfortunately, some people get stuck on the good D/P and become blind to everything else in front of them.

If you're really serious about the next step, take your time in getting to know someone, but most importantly, before you do that, take an inventory of yourself and be honest with the person in the mirror about your intentions and expectations before inviting someone into your un/occupied space. See, it's not just about having a soul mate but also a purpose and destiny mate. *"Can two walk together except they be agreed" (Amos 3:3 KJB).*

Ladies, don't feel guilty if they say you passed over a "good man." You just don't fit on his rack.

Fellas, don't feel bad if they try to bash you about passing up a "good woman." She's just not your rib!

Don't get me wrong, I don't believe that there's just "one person" in the world for you, because God is bigger than Baskin-Robbins' thirty-one flavors. You do have choices, and the selection is wonderful. You just need to find the right fit.

When that time comes, I want a man to love me at first sight, meaning I want him to *agape* (divine), to love me the way God commanded him to, unconditionally! To not judge me on my past or highlight my flaws but to see me beyond me and to love my imperfection (I'm five feet three inches; don't wish I was taller). So with this kind of love, acknowledge that I am human and I will make mistakes, yet understand that there's always room for improvement.

I want him to *phileo* (brotherly), to love me like a friend, to be affectionate toward me, meaning open up to me, talk to me, tell me his dreams and his fears, what keeps him up at night, and what gives him the strength to get up in the morning and do it all over again. I want him to see me as the person he can trust when it seems like the world is against him and he has no one else to turn to. Communication is the key in every relationship. I want him to feel like there is nothing he can't talk to me about, that he would never have to turn to another ear for attention. It's like the Word states: "A friend that sticks closer than a brother." I want us to be able to laugh at the crazy things in life and talk trash to each other. We can be rivals when it comes to sports. We don't have to like the same team, but he better respect mine! Miami all the way!

I want him to *eros* (flesh), not just see me physically but to also touch my soul with his love, to crave me, and to desire me. I want him to want me like I am the only woman on the planet. I want him to romance me, to know that I am his and he is mine, and to know that with this love, his passion will run deep. He will not hold back his love from me but will deposit everything he has in me. I want to melt in his arms to where the two of us become one. I want him to helplessly need me. I want his lust for me to be legal! Yes, I want it all. I want it the way God intended it for me to be. *"Marriage is honorable in all, and the bed undefiled"* (Heb. 13:4a). He'll be my king and I'll be his queen!

I want that kind of love where he chases me down the beach just to give me hugs and kisses.

The kind where he offers me a foot rub because he knew I've been on my feet all day.

I want that let's-relax-by-the-fireplace-and-roast-some-marshmallows kind of love.

That baby-we-don't-have-to-go-out-let's-cook-together kind of love.
We-can-disagree-but-let's-work-it-out-no-need-to-sleep-on-the-sofa kind of love.
That boy-you-get-on-my-last-never kind of love.

I want that we-don't-have-to-wait-for-the-weekend-to-have-a-good-time kind of love.

That let's-talk-on-the-phone until-we-fall-to-sleep kind of love . . . Ah, that hang-up-no-you-hang-up kind of love!

That it's-raining-let's-play-hokey-from-work kind of love . . . Shhh!
A love that is pure and healthy kind of *love*!

Song of Solomon 1:2 ESV

2 Let him kiss me with the kisses of his mouth! For your love is better than wine.

Song of Solomon 4:1–7 ESV

1 Behold, you are beautiful my love, behold you are beautiful! Your eyes are doves behind your veil. Your hair is like a flock of goats leaping down the slopes of Gilead

2 Your teeth are like a flock of shorn ewes that have come up from the washing, all of which bear twins, and not one among them has lost its young.

3 Your lips are like a scarlet thread and your mouth is lovely. Your cheeks are like halves of a pomegranate behind your veil.

4 Your neck is like the tower of David, built in rows of stone; on it hang a thousand shields, all of them shields of warriors.

5 Your two breasts are like two fawns, twins of a gazelle, that graze among the lilies. 6 Until the day breathes and the shadows flee, I will go away to the mountain of myrrh and the hill of frankincense. 7 You are altogether beautiful, my love; there is no flaw in you.

FYI: See, the Bible isn't boring! You'd be surprised of what you'd find in there if you'd only pick it up and read it!

CHAPTER 20

FORGIVENESS IS FREEDOM

By the time I hit my teenage years, my father and I didn't get along like we used to. Crazy, considering I used to be a daddy's girl! I believe it all started when I realized what he was doing behind my mother's back and I didn't like it!

The first incident I recall was when he took my brother to his girlfriend's house. My brother told us about it, and I told my mom, and she confronted him about it! I'm not sure but I think it was at that point where I became public enemy number one.

There was a time when the money went missing out of my mom's purse, and as a child, that's one thing you didn't do and get caught! *Ha*! Anyway, the money came up missing and she accused us of taking it! So I told her (I was honest), "Look, I took fifty cents. However, your husband was in your purse also!" And again, she confronted him about it, and he confronted me! Hey, I was a child. I was told to tell the truth!

SOME OF MY TRYING MOMENTS

One day, I was sitting outside on the sidewalk on a soda cracker can with my head on my lap. I think I was around thirteen at the time and I heard a voice say, "Get up." And when I lifted my head, I saw this car coming toward me, so I jumped up and moved out of the way, only for the car to run over the can I was sitting on. I was thinking, "That car almost hit me!" My dad got out of that car and just looked at me! No apology, no "Hey, are you okay?" Nothing. He just went into the house like nothing happened, while I stood there shaking, looking at the can!

As children, we loved playing around in the neighborhood! (Those were the days when children went outside and played.) Anyway, we lived in a duplex and the unit next door to us was empty. So one particular day, we went next door and played around, running up and down, screaming, scaring each other (oh, the good old days) like, you know, just being children. When my dad came home, he saw some of the children running around and told everyone to get out of the house! On the way out, I realized I left my shoes, so I went back to get them because there was no way I was going to let him catch me without shoes on my feet. (The last time he caught me without any shoes on, my feet was smashed with a baseball bat.) As I was putting them on, my dad came in and asked, "Are you disrespecting me?" and I said, "No, I left my shoes, so I came back to put them on!" He then said to me, "Oh, oh, so you think you're grown . . . " Then he grabbed me and started punching me like a dude, and at that moment, I'm thinking to myself . . . *"What did I do to deserve this?"*

I'm looking back, thinking, even as a parent, if your child did something that you disapprove of, you shouldn't punch them in their face, especially a young girl. In addition, you don't hold a grudge and try to hurt them every chance you get!

However, when I got away, I ran as fast as I could all the way up to the senior high school. I sat on the stairway leading to the catwalk, crying and confused, thinking, "What I am going to do?" After a while, I saw one of my friends walking by and I stopped her and asked if she didn't mind to stop by the house and pick up my shoes. "Yes, I left with no shoes on my feet." By the time she brought them back to me, I saw my dad coming up behind her and I took off running again! I ran so fast, I forgot I still didn't have my shoes. I ran across that catwalk over Sixty-second Street, through the park, past the pool, over the other catwalk by the high school, then past the elementary that went over I-95, all the way to my cousin's house in the projects! And I didn't stop until I got there. I stayed there for a few days until my mother came to pick me up.

If my brother or sisters did something wrong, it was my fault. If the kitchen wasn't clean (even though we took turns cleaning it), it was still my fault. I could do nothing right in his eyes! It's one thing to go to school and deal with bullies just about every day, but to come home where I should find comfort and peace, I had to deal with my father treating me like the gum on the bottom of his shoe, and it was starting to get the best of me! There was no peace in the home as far as I was concerned. It got to the point where we lived in the same house and didn't speak to each other.

I remember him fussing at me and calling me a dog, and then he said to me, "No, you're not a dog, you're a cat! Cats only hang around because you feed them!" I thought, "*Wow*! Really! Is that not what a father is supposed to do—feed, clothe, and take care of his children?" Things got so bad that I even considered suicide because I was sick of the abuse. There was no pleasing that man. Nope, I could do nothing right!

At this phase in life, my parents purchased a new home and we're now living on Forty-ninth Street and Miami. On this day, my sisters and I were in the bedroom cleaning, but my sister Dee was in my parents' room talking to one of the boys in the neighborhood (Nathanial). Meanwhile, my dad was in the backyard painting something he made (carpenter). Well, after my sister left their bedroom, he came into my room and asked me what I was doing talking to a boy through his bedroom window! Now, if you know my dad, talking to any boy was a no-no, so talking to one through his bedroom window while he was home was like having a death wish. So I told him it wasn't me! So he gets upset and asks me if I was calling him a liar. And I replied, "No, but it wasn't me." Mind you, I'm less than ninety pounds and my sister . . . well, let's just say she was "very visible," so I don't know how he couldn't differentiate between the two of us. Nevertheless, we're now going back and forward: "It wasn't me, it was Dee . . ."

Unfortunately, he would not let it go. He then asked if he was blind. I said, "No!" Now, in my mind, I'm thinking, but under my breath, I said, "Some people are so stupid!" Then I heard him say, "Did you just call me stupid?" Now, I feel some type of way because I didn't realize I said it out of my mouth, and he heard it! And the next thing I knew, he slapped me with the paintbrush that was in his hand. When I touched my face, I felt something wet, and when I looked at my hand, I thought I was bleeding. Before I knew it, I drew back a knob and I punched him in the face, and it was on and popping after that. When I realized what I did, I ran and locked myself in the bathroom, thinking, "*Oh Lawd, what did I just do?*" I should have said goodbye to my siblings because this man is going to kill me! With nowhere else to go, I climbed up on the toilet, jumped through that little bathroom window, and yes, I took off running! It took me a minute to get to my cousin's house this time because we had moved farther away, but I made it.

I was tired between him and dealing with the kids in school. I couldn't take it anymore. I asked my mom to sign me up for Job Corp and I left.

NOT MY WILL

When I got saved (gave my life to Christ), I felt like I had my ducks in a row. I was so proud of myself! I wanted to live for God and do everything he wanted me to do. One day, sitting at home after my personal Bible study, I asked the Lord a question! (Be careful what you ask for, they say!) Well, according to the Word, it says . . .

Be careful of nothing, but in everything by pray and supplication with thanksgiving let your request be made known unto God, and the peace of God that which passeth all understanding shall keep your hearts and minds through Christ Jesus (Phil. 4:6, 7). KJV

Nevertheless, I asked God if there was anything in me that would hinder my walk with him, and without hesitation, he replied: "Unforgiveness." I said, "What?" And he replied again: Unforgiveness! He said, "You need to forgive your father!" And without hesitation, I replied, "Lord, is there anything else?" because I did *not* want to forgive him for how he treated me. I literally hated that man. Nevertheless, that thing weighted heavily on me for months, thinking I really do hate this man and I didn't want to let go of the bitterness. I fought with that for a long time yet, thinking this man can hinder my walk with the Lord! After months of contemplating, I decided to reach out to my mother and asked her to reach out to him.

Now, when I tell you it took everything in me to forgive this man, I mean it! Because in the beginning, I only forgave him with my mouth! Yeah, let's just say "the words of my mouth and the meditation of my heart" were not acceptable, according to Psalms 19:14! My heart was still far from it. Forgiving him didn't come easily because we all have that one thing in common called "memory," so the memories started talking to me, reminding me of all the pain he's caused me, and those memories were overriding the voice of God.

I was in a panic of fear, but I still didn't want to let go, hoping God would change his mind and allow this one to slide because of all he put me through! At one point, I was hoping death would come early, just so I wouldn't have to forgive him! Crazy, I know, but that's how much I wanted to hate him. Thank God, he had a better plan. Trust me when I tell you this was not an easy journey, like I said, and no, it didn't happen overnight. It took a lot of praying and fasting, in addition to reading God's word! I would say with my mouth that I forgave him, but in my heart, I still had some work to do! The fight continued, but I was getting better.

One year, I was in the process of filing for my citizenship and the officer needed a copy of both my parents' citizenship documents. My mom sent her papers, but he didn't. His reason for not sending it, you asked? Well, he told my mother whom I called and said, "Hey, send me your citizenship paper." He claimed that I didn't say hello, no "how are you doing?" just "Send me your citizenship papers!" Now, how does that even sound? Crazy, right, I know! One thing if nothing else my parents taught us to be respectful of others, always say good morning, afternoon, or evening when you walk into a room. Never interrupt a conversation, wait for people to stop talking to say what you need to say, and when calling someone's home, always be polite. Therefore, these things stayed with me throughout my life even until now. So, for him to use that as an excuse for him not to send the papers was not a good one! Needless to say, my application was denied and $700 went down the drain, so you know I was l livid. I had to pay an additional $200 if I wanted to appeal, or wait five more years to reapply, so yes, I was *hott* and yes, with two *T*s! At this point, my forgiveness is being tested again, not worth going to hell for, but OMG, tempting! I did not want to talk to him, look at him, or hear his name.

And when ye stand to pray, forgive, if ye have aught against any: that your Father also which is in heaven may forgive you your trespasses. But if you do not forgive, neither will your Father which is in heaven forgive your trespasses (Mark 11:25–26, KJV).

Truth be told, that scripture was not something I wanted to hear, and it felt like a horse pill that someone was shoving down my throat and I didn't want to swallow it. I came this close to kicking a hole in the wall, but I didn't! Well, not this time! Can you see how *awesome* God is? He delivered someone like me! Thinking, I wonder if this is one of the reasons some people don't have a prayer life, because they don't want to forgive! Just thinking!

To shorten this story, through the process of time, I finally, from the depth of my heart, forgave him, not so much for him but I did it also for me. I realize I couldn't go too far in the kingdom with hate and unforgiveness in my heart, and the truth is, the Lord showed me some things about me that he wasn't so pleased with, and that I was also in need of being forgiven.

As humans, we are so quick to focus on how people hurt us, not realizing that we sometimes hurt others as well. As my bishop would say, "When you change the way you look at things, the things you look at will change!"

Now, thirty-plus years later and my dad is battling with prostate cancer. The cancer is also in his bones. In addition to that, he's a diabetic and recently had a stroke! Wow, the enemy tried to get me to believe he's going through this because he was a "bad father," but I had to rebuke him in the name of Jesus and let him know that I don't know why God is allowing him to go through this, but I know that my God is a healer and a keeper.

If I ever doubted if I really forgave him, it was at that moment. For years, as an intercessor, I dealt with spiritual warfare, especially in my dreams, to the point where I was afraid to go to sleep. As an intercessor, I have access to the certain realm in the spirit, that's why it's important for me to be led by the spirit. When my sisters called and said the doctors had sent him home to die, I had to brace myself because I knew even though my father confessed salvation (I asked him), I also knew he was not ready to die. The spirit of fear was so heavy that I felt it in every word he spoke.

During that week, I had a dream that my dad came to visit me. When he walked into my bedroom, he stood tall and confident. He looked strong like there was nothing wrong with him. I took notice of everything about him. He didn't say a word; he just looked at me, playing with the baby (I don't know whose baby it was). Nevertheless, he just smiled, then he turned and walked away, going back toward the living room. A few minutes later, he came back and stood by my bedroom door, but this time he was short, hungover, and sickly looking, and I thought, what happened? He was doing just fine a few minutes ago! I went behind him as I was asking him what happened, but he didn't say a word. Nevertheless, I continued to follow him as he walked through my guest bedroom, thinking that's not an exit!

But when I went through the door, I was standing outside on a porch. The room turned into a balcony porch, and the air was gloomy with the mist of soft rain. As I was going behind him, the Spirit said, "Stop, don't leave the porch," so I stood there, holding on to the railing, calling out to him to come back. I cried so hard, screaming, *"Daddy, come back, Daddy, come back,"* but it was like he didn't hear a word I said as he was walking away! As I stood there watching him, he had transformed again. This time, he stood tall in stature as he walked down the sidewalk, whistling as if he didn't have a care in the world, but I continued to cry out to him: *"Daddy, please come back."* I almost felt out of breath, and then, like a vapor, he vanished into the air, and just like that, he was gone! I woke up and my heart was racing for only God knows how fast. I sat on my bed thinking I need to pray. So, in addition to my regular prayer, I had to add fasting and target him in prayer! My prayer was to pray the will of my earthly father's desires! Why do you ask?

"Therefore I tell you, whatever you ask in prayer, believe that you have received it, and it will be yours" (Mark 11:24, ESV).

And since I knew my father wasn't ready to die, I decided to stand with him in prayer. How do I know that he wasn't ready? Well, one of the reasons is they wanted to send him to a hospice for final care, and he told them, "That's where you send people to die!" So, that's one of the reasons I knew he wasn't ready, and that is why I stood in prayer with him!

"We then that are strong ought to bear the infirmities of the weak, and not to please ourselves" (Rom. 15:1, KJV).

So, you see, it's not always about us. This has happened on more than one occasion. I'm not crazy because I know that one day, death will come, but my prayer is "God, don't take him with the spirit of pride and fear present. Let him know beyond the shadows of death that when he closes his eyes, he will be at peace, knowing that he will wake up in your arms." Even as believers, sometimes there's this uneasiness about going to the other side that can grip at us. I don't care how "saved or spiritual" you think you are! Death will show up at your door if Jesus doesn't delay his coming.

This is one of the reasons *forgiveness* is so important. At the end of the day, it's not about you, but God getting the glory out of you! That was over four years ago. At the beginning of this year, he was going back and forth to the hospital, and I would drive down to Miami to check up on him. But back in April, my family called and said the hospital released him to home hospice. My prayer at the time was, "Lord, not my will!" I felt a release in my spirit, so that weekend, I decided to drive down one more time, because you never know. He was asleep when I got there, so I just sat, watched him, and prayed within myself.

The family came and went, and some of them talked as if he was already dead. But again, I just watched. They said his mind was far gone and that he didn't remember anyone, but when he woke up in pain, I stood by his bed and rubbed his body, trying to bring a little comfort, telling him it was going to be okay. When he heard my voice, he turned, looked at me, and called my name, asking if it was me, and I said yes! He tried talking, but I told him to relax and I stood there rubbing his arms and legs.

The next day, I went back over there and just sat with him, and again watching the family coming and going. By the end of the night, as I sat and watched him, I told myself that I need to do something. I then took the oil from my purse, began to anoint his body, and prayed over him. All this time, I thought he was sleep, but when I was done, he looked at me and said, *"Thank you!"* Honestly, I was shocked but glad to know that he appreciated it! The next day, my job called, so I had to come back to Jacksonville. Three days later, he went to sleep! Rest in peace, Jacob Jones!

Looking back over my life, I now understand why it was so hard for me to trust and believe God. The name "father" paralyzed me! I couldn't trust and depend on my earthly father, so how was I going to trust my Heavenly Father when it looked like he had forsaken me as well? Where was God when I needed him the most? Where was he when it seemed like all hell broke loose in my life? If I was being tested, this was the longest test in history, because it seemed like every time I came out of one thing, I was going back into something else. In addition, I didn't get the love and affection I needed from my father, neither security nor protection. So how do I make the transition from my earthly father over to my Heavenly Father without feeling the sting? When my father and mother forsake me, then the Lord will take me up (Ps. 27:10). Well, let's just say the transition wasn't that easy.

I told myself I had faith in God, but the words that came out of my mouth said something else. I honestly didn't trust God like I thought I did. Because when I was faced with difficulty, I was doing more begging and pleading with God than asking. I did not ask in faith because I did not know how to operate in faith. My strongest faith was me believing God for salvation. Mostly, everything else was hoping and crossing my fingers.

It took years for God to get me to the place where I could say that I trust and believe him, because it seemed like every time I "trusted and believed God for something," I was left disappointed and let down. I would cry out in prayer, "Lord, I trusted you for this" or "I believed you for that," but what I prayed for never happened! It didn't work in my favor. I guess God knew deep down I really didn't trust him, and just like my earthly father, I knew he would let me down and I somewhat blame him for how my life turned out! After all, he's God. He knows and sees everything! He's omnipotent, all-powerful, almighty, supreme. He's able to do "anything"! He's omnipresent (everywhere at the same time) and omniscient (all-knowing), so why did he allow me to go through all the hell I've been through in my life? Nevertheless, like Job, I was reminded that God owed me nothing. But again, like Job, it didn't stop me from asking the million *whys*!

SHE DID IT

There was an incident that happened some years back and it really shocked a lot of people. A few young ladies were affected the most, and the person in the middle didn't seem to understand the pain she caused them or just didn't care, and I had a problem with that. Now, it was not what she did to me that caused me to feel the way I did toward her, but it was what she did to them. As a result, every time I saw her, I wanted her to know I didn't like her or what she did was wrong. Yeah, that bothered me for a very long time. One night, during prayer, the Lord said to me, "Pray for her," and I replied *no*! Because, again, I felt like what she did was wrong and I was still in disbelief, so I didn't want to pray for her.

On the next night during prayer, again, the Lord said, "Pray for her," so I was like "Okay, Lord, bless her, blah blah blah!" Still not feeling it, and from time to time, the Lord would show me her face in prayer. She would just pop up, I couldn't get away from it! So, one night during prayer, the Lord said to me, "How do you know if she didn't ask for forgiveness, and how do you know if I didn't forgive her?" When he said that, I was like well, um, mute (I had nothing), okay! That really broke me! Therefore, I had to repent and ask for "forgiveness," and yes, I began to pray for her. In doing so, I was able to let go of all the hate and bitterness I felt toward her. I don't care if you agree with me or not, forgiveness is freedom! Sometimes we must learn how let it go!

TO LOVE IS TO FORGIVE

Divorce was not a part of the plan; I'm a Christian, I love God. I was still supposed to be married, living the life I'd always dreamed. After all, God did say he would give me the desires of my heart, and my heart's desire was to be with my husband until we departed by death. So what happened? Life happened! I can't tell you why God allowed this to happen, but he did! I sometimes wonder why the Lord allows all the things that we see going on in the world every day, but only he knows why!

"For as the heavens are higher than the earth, so are my ways higher than your ways, and my thoughts than your thoughts" (Isaiah 55:9, ASV).

No doubt about it, God is still in control. Did I forgive my ex? Yes! Even though my heart was broken, I knew I had to do it. Forgiveness started in my mouth before it hit my heart. But I know my words and my heart had to come into an agreement.

"Let the words of my mouth, and the meditation of my heart be acceptable in thy sight O Lord, my strength, and my redeemer" (Ps. 19:14). KJV

I didn't do it for him; I did it for me. I did not want it to linger longer than it had to. I put my all on the altar and I allow God to heal me. I cried, I fasted, I prayed, I cried some more, fasted some more, and prayed some more. I was honest with myself about how I felt. I did not live in denial and I did not allow people to put me in a box. I had friends that I could talk to and I was as transparent with them as I could be because I wanted to be free from all the pain. Now, I can honestly say it took some time, but God did it! I have a newfound freedom that I never thought was possible.

"To appoint unto them that mourn in Zion, to give unto them beauty for ashes, the oil of joy for mourning, the garment of praise for the spirit of heaviness; that they might be called trees of righteousness, the planting of the Lord, that he might be glorified" (Isa. 61:3, KJV).

We must realize that we all need forgiveness. It's like a revolving door—you're either giving it or receiving it, and it is continual!

EXERCISE

So, why do we forgive?

1. We do it because God commands us to!
2. Because it frees us from keeping people locked away in our minds, and it allows us to release them and set them free.

Now, I dare to ask you, who are you holding hostage and why? Let's start the forgiving process. First, forgive yourself for whatever it is you feel guilty about, then ask God for forgiveness to let it go.

I _____

Forgive _____

For _____

_____

_____

_____

_____

_____

_____

Don't let it stop here. If there's someone else you need to forgive, get a blank sheet of paper and get to writing.

Forgiveness is not just for the other person; it's also for you. Once you learn to forgive, you can free yourself from all the pain and frustration that that person or people caused you. But most importantly, you bring glory to God, because what you're saying is, "God, I trust you in this pain and I know you will deliver me from all the hurt." It is the devil's job to keep you in bondage (stop employing him), so don't think you're hurting the person by not forgiving them. You will only continue to hurt the person in the mirror!

CHAPTER 21

CAN WE TALK SISTER-TO-SISTER?

I'm a woman, so let me speak to the ladies for just a second. Sisters, respect yourself and know your worth. Every man that screams "I love you," heck, well, these days say "I like you," is not entitled to your jewels. I'm not telling you how to live your life, but what I will say is this: If you must, make him responsible. I'm not promoting premarital sex. I wish to God that you would wait, but some people are going to do what they want to do no matter what you say, because, yeah, I know, "you're grown." However, if I could grab your ear, and I don't even need both of them, for about 2.5 seconds, hear me, please. So again, I say, make him responsible—use protection.

A one-minute, okay, two-minute orgasm is not worth a lifetime of HIV treatments. My bishop said something years ago and it stayed with me. He said, "While approaching a *red* light, you have to make a decision. You can stop and wait for it to turn green, then proceed, or you can run right through it. Now, in running the red light, you need to deal with the consequences. Granted you might run through it and nothing happens, cool, you're in the clear. However, you can also run through it and cause a collision that may cause injuries to yourself or an innocent bystander." You have the power to make the right decision, but the consequences are not yours to make. To every action, there's a reaction, so please *think*!

A man that really loves and respects you will wait on you. Most importantly, the man that God has for you! There are so many lies the enemy is whispering into the ears of women to make them give it up. One is "If you don't do it, another woman will." Really, boy? Bye! If that's the case, let her, and you go find someone else. Or better yet, wait on God to send the right person into your life who will appreciate you and respect your decision to wait because he never loved you in the first place. Stop giving the men ammunition to use against you! Remember, it's he that finds a wife. Allow God to present you to your husband like he presented Eve to Adam! Wait on being someone's good thing and not someone's plaything!

Try this the next time a man says, "I want to make love to you." Just scream with excitement, saying, "Yes, I'll marry you," then pick up the phone, call your girlfriends, and say "OMG, we're getting married . . ." If he says, "Hold up, wait a minute, I didn't say anything about getting married," then you say, "What_____?"

Now, the floor is open for discussion, if you haven't already, where this relationship is going! If his love is only limited to the bedroom, then that's not the love you're looking for—that's lust!

Watch out for the man who doesn't bring you around his family or friends, but only want to hang around you when it's convenient. Don't fall for that "I like to keep my relationship private." No, he wants to keep you private. I can understand that for a few weeks, in the getting-to-know-you process, but if you decide to commit, then you need to get to know some of the people in his world!

Bump that Netflix and chill crap. When is the next family-and-friends BBQ? Stop selling yourself short. Any man that wants to be with you will not have a problem introducing you to his family and friends. Besides, you need to see how he interacts with others. Is he one way with you and another with them, or is he consistent?

Believe it or not, there are some men out there that know their worth too. Not every man is paralyzed by a big butt and a smile. Most of these men are smarter than you think. If you give it up, some will take it with no hesitation!

By the way, there's nothing wrong with you asking your partner "what's in their closet." Not saying that they're homosexual, but rather finding out what can hinder the relationship from going forward when considering a life partner.

For example:

Are you holding on to your first love? If he/she walked back into your life, would you consider leaving the person you're pursuing?

How many people are you still tied too?
Did you divorce ex from your soul or are there still some soul ties?
Are you still spiritually connected?
On a scale of one to ten, how jealous are you?
Are there any exes or baby mommas that still want you back? Let's talk about that!

These are just a few things to consider when thinking about inviting someone into your life. Ask them as well as yourself! If you're not honest with yourself, just about everything you tell a person is a lie because you're hiding the truth. Go back to your "prayer closet" and ask God to reveal your hidden secrets that are buried in the back of your mind. In essence, clean your house before inviting someone over!

I would even dare to say get tested (STD/HIV). Don't be afraid to know your status. "They say what you don't know won't hurt you, but the truth of the matter is, what you don't know can kill you and someone else," so don't be careless, get tested! This way, neither you nor your partner will be in the dark.

If you're sexually active and never had an HIV/STD test, you need to *stop*! You should *not* be having sex. Go get tested. I know it might be a little scary, but go get it done! I remember the first time I went, I was shaking in my booth and I didn't have any on. I was scared to death. But I told myself, regardless of the outcome, you still need to know! I'm not sexually active, but I still get it done every year. I'm still nervous when I do, but I have to! If I had it, I would stay single for the rest of my life (unless God says otherwise) than have it and not know and cause harm to someone else.

If you're afraid to ask your partner about their last HIV/STD test status, you should *not* be in that relationship or have sex with them!

If your partner gets offended because you asked for an HIV/STD test, you should definitely *not* be having sex.

I believe that you both should get tested before getting married. Some people are willing to stick with you and take the necessary precautions if they know ahead of time, but if not, let them walk away. I know it will hurt, but you'll be okay! God got you! So please protect yourself and do us all a favor and get tested. This is for both men and women.

Now, I know that this might come as a surprise to some of you, so hold your horses, okay? Guess what? "I wasn't saved all my life!" There, I said it! I know, I know, but yes, it's true!

Before Christ/salvation, I used to implement the "three-month rule" too! But when I gave my life to Christ, I started implemented the "wedding-night rule," meaning I decide to remain abstinent until I got married. However, I didn't think it would take fifteen years before I got married. (I know some of you just fainted.) But truth be told, it was not as hard as you think. Okay, I'm lying. It was hard! Lord knows I had some moments, but as time went on, it got a little easier! Number one reason was because I asked God to keep me because I wanted to be kept. Therefore, I got involved in ministry! You name it, I probably did it: prison ministry, altar workers ministry, dance ministry, outreach ministry, new members orientation, Sunday school teacher . . . One of the main ministries that kept me grounded was being a youth leader. There was no way I could tell the young people to abstain and I was "in between the sheets." It was not a "Do as I say," but rather "Do what I do."

Some men are quick to say nobody's going to marrying a woman before sleeping with her (lies), just like nobody's going to purchase a vehicle without test-driving it! Well, pumpkin, let me clean your glasses so that you can clearly see that I'm not a car, so there will be no test-driving. For the record, anybody can go on a car lot and test-drive a Honda, Toyota, Nissan, or Kia, and you might even be able to test-drive a BMW or Lexus. Come to think of it, do you know that there are people who go to car lots just to test-drive a car, yet have no intention of purchasing one? All they wanted to do was enjoy the ride for a moment, then return it. Now, the car has unnecessary mileages only because someone wanted to go for a joyride. Don't be no one's joyride! Nevertheless, what you need to do is get away from me with that foolishness because, again, I am not a car. Furthermore, if you're going to drive something, drive something that's been qualified. I might not know much, but I do know you're not going to walk on a lot and "test-drive" an Aston Martin Valkyrie, a Bugatti Chiron, a Lamborghini, or a Ferrari! Trust and believe that they're not going to just give you the keys and let you, as you put it, "test-drive," because you will need to prove that you're worthy to even hold the keys. Can you afford a Lamborghini or a Ferrari, in addition to the others listed? If not, how dare you think you can just get in the car and go for a drive just to say you took it for a spin! (All things being equal.) Not today, devil, not today! Hold up . . . What did you say, sis? Did I hear you say, "Jesus, take the wheel?" Oh okay, well, since he's in the driver seat, the only way for you to get in that seat is for him to get out, and Jesus is not giving up his seat just so you can go for a joyride!

Here's another one . . . I need to test the waters before jumping in the ocean. First of all, half of you can't ever swim in a pool, talking about jumping in the ocean. Besides, do you know how big the ocean is? Do you really think you can swim that long? Not!

Now, if you want to compare me to something, why not make it a *house*? You see, you may get a tour, but you're not moving in without a down payment and at least a thirty-year mortgage.

Ladies, you must demand respect. Don't sell yourself short because you don't want to be alone. Enjoy this time with God, your family, and friends. Trust me, the man that God has for you is for you, and he will respect your decision to wait. In the meantime and in between time, work on being a better you!

OH BROTHER

Okay, men, I'm not going to throw y'all under the bus because I know there are some women out there that are putting the pressure on you as well, challenging your manhood, as you would put it, but it doesn't make you less of a man for wanting to wait. I applaud you and I pray for your strength in the Lord. Be the man God has called you to be, and I know in due season he will return your rib. Besides, the Word does say, "He that finds a wife" and remember, when you find her, you will also find "*favor*"!

CHAPTER 22

WAIT ON THE LORD

"They that wait!" The question on the floor is: How do you wait on the Lord?

There's a song that the choir used to sing pertaining to "waiting on the Lord." At first I would sing along, but as time went on, I developed a love-hate relationship with that song because the lyrics became loud in my ear and I realized that, hey, I'm waiting on God to do some things and they haven't happened yet! How much longer do I have to wait?

"But they that wait upon the Lord shall renew their strength; they shall mount up like wings as eagles; they shall run, and not be weary, and they shall walk and not faint" (Isa. 40:31). ESV

To renew is to repeat, give fresh life or strength to, or replace something that was broken or worn out, according to the dictionary!

*What do you do when you're waiting on God and it seems like he's nowhere to be found? When you fasted and prayed, and prayed and fasted, but it feels like all you did was miss a meal?

*What do you tell yourself after you stepped out on faith, stood on his word, and spoke and declared his word according to James 1:6? *"But let him ask in faith, with no doubting, for the one who doubts is like a wave of the sea that is driven and tossed by the wind." ESV* And with all that faith, all that fasting, all of that praying, you have *nothing* to show for it! Where is *God*? I'm tired, I'm frustrated, I told people God was going to fix it. Now, here I am and people are looking at me like, "Where's your God again?" And If I hear one more "I told you so," they're going to feel my wrath because I'm done! Well, are you?

"And David was greatly distressed, for the people spoke of stoning him, because all the people were bitter in soul, each for his sons and daughters. But David strengthened (encouraged) himself in the Lord his God" (1 Sam. 30:6).

Even in your waiting, you must learn to encourage yourself. I don't care what you're waiting on or believing God for. Remember *Ecclesiastes 3:1 (AMP): There is a season (a time appointed) for everything and a time for every delight and event or purpose under heaven.* Delayed doesn't mean denied!

So what does it mean to wait? Okay, to wait on God means to get busy on the assignment that God has given you. Get busy on things in the kingdom!

One scripture comes to mind.

Ecclesiastes 9:10a ESV: Whatever your hand finds to do, do it with all your might!

Therefore, get busy living, get busy in the ministry, and get busy enjoying your family and friends. What is it that you're passionate about? Get busy doing that! Change the way you look at doing things. Have you taken a vacation yet? Oh, you don't know where to go . . . Look, take a few days off, drive down to the next city, rent a room, and pack a few books if you need to! Just get away from your norm! Waiting on God is not standing still—that's waiting on a bus. Before you know it, the things you've been praying for will begin to manifest. Yes, the blessings will run you over.

Amos 9:13: Yes indeed, it won't be long now God's decree "Things are going to happen so fast your head will swim, one thing fast on the heels of the other. You won't be able to keep up. Everything will be happening at once and everywhere you look, blessings! Blessings like wine pouring off the mountains and hills."

If you stay with God, he will give you the strength you need to run this race. In time, he will give you the desires of your heart (his heart), but what he's not going to do is just give you anything that would cause you to self-destruct.

I would love for him to just give me the winning lottery number, but hey, that's just me. For some of you, you're just not ready (mentally, physically, or emotionally). God is still working on the inside of you to get all that junk out of you, but when he's done, you shall come forth as pure gold. The word states that *there's nothing he would withhold from them who walk uprightly before him.* So don't get distracted by what you see. Just continue to keep believing, obeying, serving, and trusting God, and in due season, you will reap if you don't faint.

See, here's the thing. Oftentimes, when people speak about singles, most of them think, "Oh, they just want to get married." Now, in some cases, that's true. However, that's not the only thing we think about. There's a bigger world out there.

We also worry about our jobs, bills, going back to school to further our education, ministry, and the list goes on, not to mention the single parents and all they must focus on. Yeah, I know married people have the same issue, but the Bible does say that "two are better that one." Therefore, you're not going at it alone; you have help! And if you don't, something is wrong! So, basically, what I'm saying is, marriage is not the only thing on our minds. Oh, and if it was, *so what?*

Furthermore, everyone is not having the same experience in a single villa. I know it sounds crazy, but some people actually like being single and they're happy and contented!

TELL THE TRUTH, SHAME THE DEVIL

John 8:7 NIV When they kept on questioning him, he straightened up and said to them, "Let anyone of you who is without sin be the first to throw a stone at her."

So, before you throw your rock at me, look in your own closet. I said earlier that I was abstinent for fifteen years before I got married. Although I would love to tell you that every day was peaches and cream, I must admit they weren't. Now, in the beginning was smooth sailing because all I wanted to do was please the Lord. I stayed busy in ministry during those first seven to eight years.

Altar worker/intercessory prayer, choir, dance ministry, outreach ministry, new members orientation, prison ministry, Sunday school teacher, singles ministry, usher, and youth leader.

Although I had my moments, they did not overtake me. I was focused! For the record, I was not in all of these at once, but 5/6 at one time. I remember a friend asking me "Is there anything you don't do in the church?" Everything about me was about the kingdom. I was gung-ho!

As time went on, pastor decided to limit the members to at least three ministries at one time because he felt like there were too many members for only a handful of people to be doing all the work. So now, my focus is on the altar worker/ intercessory prayer, prison ministry, and ushering. It felt weird not being as busy as I was!

One day at work, some of the ladies were having a conversation during a break, and one of the ladies mentioned how she loved to please her husband. I'm intrigued because I've never heard anyone spoke so boldly and passionate as she did. She talked about how she would show up to her husband's job, meet in the back seat, and do what she wanted to do. "Oral" application was her favorite, as she puts it. I thought, "How gross," but I was still intrigued, so I continued to listen. I've never heard women talk about this; it was considered taboo especially in the church! As I continued to listen, she went on to say she loved it so much that she would even give classes on it if she could, and that they even have classes online. I was like, really, wow! (Be very careful of what you let in to your spirit.) The question got to me, and I expressed that I never participated in "oral" application. As I was growing up, that was considered something bad girls did. You were called a chicken head or a hoe, not a whore, where I'm from. I didn't want to be called as such, so it was a no for me. Besides, I thought it was nasty. Some thought I was being funny, but I was dead serious! We would continue to have our little discussions in the cubicle during our breaks. It wasn't always about sex, but when the topic came up, it wasn't one to be overlooked.

As time went on, I thought about those conversations, and as new people came into my life, I began to discover that it was not as taboo as I thought. However, I'm still the only one not in the loop (girl talk), yet I was fine with that. Besides, I'm still single. So, one day, the question was asked: "So, what are you going to do if that's something your husband likes, are you still not going to do it?" That's when I got spiritual: "God's not going to send me someone who likes that if he knows I don't do it!" So, now I'm thinking again: What if this is something my husband wants, would I deny him? Yes, yes, I would deny him because that is just nasty. I just couldn't seem to bring myself to believing I had to do such a thing.

Months gone by and I'm sitting at home one day and I logged in to my BlackPlanet account (don't worry if you don't know what that is). Anyways, I got a pop-up, and that pop-up took me back to the conversations we had in the cubicle. So, I thought, would it hurt to investigate what the "oral application" was all about? Naaa, I'll pass, not my thing. However, the thought would come to me from time to time. Is it wrong? I don't know, but I felt some type-away about it, so I started going back and forward in my mind! What's the big deal? You're not going to do it, but curiosity was knocking at my door! What if this is something my husband really likes, is it wrong to want to know how it's done? According to my coworker, there's a right and a wrong way to do it.

Now, here I was, sitting in front of the computer surfing the net and I decided that I would investigate it. I was kind of nervous. I didn't know how to word it, so I played around with words just to see what would come up. Then, boom, I did it and now I'm in another world. I clicked on one thing, and one thing leads to another, and another, and another, and I'm like, wait a minute, that's not what I was looking for, but now I can't look away! Growing up, I saw Playboy magazines, but they were just pictures. This is a whole lot more—its sex, sex, and more sex, not just pictures, but videos too! I was only looking for oral, so how did I end up looking at all of this? It was like I was trapped. Now, my flesh is starting to wake up like someone was knocking hard on my door and now I want to explore, but I can't. I'm still single, so what am I to do? There's nothing I can do, or is there? . . . Nooooo, no, no, I can't, but I want to, but I can't . . . Now, I'm sexually frustrated. My hormones are off the charts and I need some release, but I'm still single. What am I going to do? Nothing. Pray, pray, pray is what I told myself! Yeah, okay, I'm praying, but my lower body is throbbing!

Oh, Lord, what did I do? Now, she wakes and I'm horny and can't seem to find a release. Mind you, this was not in one day; it went off and on for a few months. I was really fighting with this! One day, Regina came home while I was online and the computer froze (it was old) and I just knew she was going to catch me. The door opened and I hear Regina say, "August, whatcha doing?" Meanwhile, I'm in the room trying to get the computer to unfreeze. Now normally, she would go straight to her room, but this time she came into the computer room and looked at the computer. As soon as she looked at it, I hit the off button on the hard drive! That was close, I thought to myself, but I believed she saw it!

Masturbation was never something I cared for and I still don't! However, during that time, I found myself curious, but something in me was pulling me back. It just felt dirty, but it didn't stop me from watching porn. I know it might sound crazy, but it was mostly to learn some things in case I needed it for my future husband. But my flesh and my mind were not on one accord. So now, I'm up late at night surfing the net, and I find myself looking at it again, and this time, I felt like I was at a point of no return. Feeling disgusted and enticed at the same time, I wanted to stop, but my flesh was saying, "Who's going to know? You're not hurting anyone. Go ahead, try it . . ." No, no, no, I can't, but people naturally do it all the time.

I'm going back and forward within myself and tempting myself. Okay, August, pray. I prayed—that didn't help. It felt like my flesh was at a place of curiosity, and before I knew it, I gave in and it was shorter than a two-minute brother.

Oh Lord, what did I do?

It was a little pleasure for a second, but I cried the rest of the night! I felt ashamed and embarrassed because I felt like God was watching me. But guess what? I did it again and again. And even though I felt disgusted, I felt justified. I wasn't hurting anyone. After all, it's my body! But I found that when I did it, it paralyzed me spiritually because I would bow out when it came to ministry. I would step to the side and allow others to go forward. I didn't want to feel like I was transferring any negative spirits on to people I was praying for. I might have been selfish when it came to me, but I still had to use wisdom when it came to God's people. Every time I gave into my flesh, I asked for forgiveness, but I never repented. Oh yes, there's a difference!

As crazy as it sounds, I believe it was also part of God's plan to humble me. I never said it out loud, but I had this self-righteous attitude because I wasn't out there sleeping around. I couldn't understand why people wouldn't wait; I was waiting. I wasn't out sleeping around, so why was it so hard for others? I didn't get it. I honestly had to learn that *"everyone's"* struggle is different and is handled differently.

I would begin to hear messages on pornography or side messages on self-gratification. I would feel it was poking at me. One day, Sandra gave me a CD that Pastor Davis preached on self-fulfillment. At first I didn't want to hear it, but I knew I was seeking the truth, so I had to kill my flesh and allow my spirit to take a listen. See, this was God working, because Sandra didn't have a clue as to what I was going through and she opened to me about some of her struggles. I had to first pray and ask the Lord to speak to me, and then I had to be honest with myself and be open to what he would say!

That message really cut me deep. It took me to scriptures I never paid attention to, and he broke it down to where there was no misunderstanding. I had a decision to make, so what was I going to do? I played that CD over and over. A part of me was in disbelief, and the other part was looking for truth in the inward man.

I prayed and cried, I cried and prayed, and prayed and fast. I had to find my way back to me because the "me" I was living was not me. It was the enemy trying to take over me. Now, I'm fighting to get back to the person I once was. It didn't happen overnight, but *God* did it.

As I began to reflect, I connected the dots back to my childhood. I was unaware that the spirit was lying dormant because I never addressed it; I buried it in the back of my mind. Unfortunately, anything buried can be exhumed; however, that's not such a bad thing in this case!

Looking back, I realized I've invested too much in the kingdom to throw it all away on a technicality! Now, I must do some spiritual cleansing because I refuse to live in bondage. Again, as the bishop said, "If you don't face it, God won't heal it!"

Everyone's story is different, so again, I had to connect the dots for me. As painful as it was, I had to go back into my past and confront my demons that attacked me! I had to face the people who molested me. I didn't remember their names, but I can see their faces along with their actions. I had to let them know that they stole my life, they stole my voice, they paralyzed me, and caused me to lie to myself. I held on to secrets I should have never kept. You abused me for your own pleasure and told me it was okay when it wasn't! I didn't belong to you, yet you trespass without permission and took advantage of me. I hate you for what you made of me! *Fearful* instead of *fearless*!

I had to speak life to myself, I had to rewrite my story, I had to encourage myself. I'm not what you made of me, I'm who God says I am. I'm more than a conqueror! You picked a fight with me when I didn't know how to fight, when I didn't have the strength to resist you. I thought you took my voice until I met *Jesus*. He ministered to me; he told me to give him my pain and trust him to make me whole again. At first I didn't believe it was possible, but here I am talking about and revealing some of my deepest secret things I thought I would take to my grave because I was too embarrassed and ashamed to talk about it! You lost, devil. God won. I won. *I'm free, I'm free, I am free.*

CHAPTER 23

MY FIRST LOVE

Here I am once again, a little over a year sitting in the front row listening to people talk about how wonderful she was, listening to them sing songs, and trying to understand how I got her! Never in a million years did I thought I would be sitting here this soon, looking, thinking, and wondering if this is real or is it a dream. This can't be real was what I'm telling myself. But as I looked on, I can't help but notice that my reality is sitting in my face and it's telling me this is the last time I will see her face again. So I looked on for as long as I could to catch every picture in my mind, fighting back the tears so it won't blur my vision of what she looked like lying there, not saying a word, not looking back, just lying there! And I can't help but wonder, "Why God, why her, why now, why us?" Everybody kept saying she's in a better place or she's no longer in pain, she's not suffering anymore. My comprehension was limited, and to be honest, I really didn't want to hear any of that. I want her here with me, with us.

In my mind, I'm asking, where is God, where is the God that she trusts, where is the God that she believed can do anything, where is the God of the Bible who says, "*If you can believe all things are possible*," where is God who said that "*Healing is the children's bread,*" because all I see is my mother lying in a box and in my mind I'm still believing in God to heal her. But that's not what's happening right now because I'm saying goodbye, or better yet, see you later! I'm confused, I'm hurt, and I'm angry as____. To be honest, I was a little salty because my understanding had no understanding.

I cried myself to sleep every night. I honestly felt like dying. I cried so much to where I felt like I was going to die of a broken heart because it was just that painful!

I would sit in prayer, but I couldn't pray. And when I opened my mouth, I kept asking God why! This is beyond heartbreaking, and I was completely devastated! I continued to ask myself, where's God? I believed him for total healing, I believed that he would raise her up, and I believed that she would have a testimony. So, to just say to me that she's in no more pain was like water off a duck's back: it just didn't penetrate, it didn't do anything for my belief system. All I wanted was my mother! I wanted to see her smile again, to hear her laugh again, and hear her voice again.

She spent a year in that hospital, and every day I believe that she would get up. I prayed, I fasted, consecrated myself, and sanctified myself just to hear God's voice concerning her healing! The dreams and visions I had all pointed to her getting up. Am I crazy, was it just me? Was it just something I wanted so badly that I made myself believe it? Hours, days, and weeks went by and every hour, every day, and every week thereafter, I couldn't stop crying!

I remember getting the phone call . . . I was in total denial for hours. My sister called and said, "Mommy's heart stopped beating," and I asked her, "What they were going to do about it?" I went in my prayer closet and started talking to God, asking him to work a miracle I know he's able to, but he knew she was already gone. So, looking back, the prayer was really for me. He knew I was going to need it.

To be honest, I really don't know if I would still be walking out my salvation if it wasn't for my mother. The life she lived before me represented Christ to the fullest! The way she treated people, the way she respects her husband despite his indiscretions, the way she took people in instead of treating them as strangers! The ones I brought home, the people that my siblings brought home, the sanitation workers that came by and pick up the trash . . . it didn't matter who it was; if they were hungry, she fed them. If people came into town, she opened her doors to them, not to mention how she feeds the church!

Never in my years of living have I ever heard her use profanity. She always had a way of saying "vengeance is the Lord's" when people mistreat or misused her. She never had an "I'll get you back" mentality (so, I guess I got that from my dad). She depended on God for everything, and with every fiber of my being, she trusted him with everything in her. She prayed like no other, and her faith was undeniable! Honestly, she's the reason I am the praying woman that I am today!

Looking back, I'm trying to see what I missed. Did I not see the signs? As I reflected, I remembered all the phone conversations we had. We would be on the phone for hours as she would go down memory lane sharing with me her family history, what she experienced as a child growing up in the Turks and Caicos Islands, and things she's never shared with me before, and I was in awe just listening, and every day was something different.

She shared with me the time I was born. Even the fact that my father didn't believe that I was his child, asking if she was sure (it just goes to show that there's nothing new under the sun . . . negroes have been denying their children since the beginning of time), side-eyes rolling!

Nevertheless, one night I was driving home after leaving a restaurant listening to The Special Formula live music (very talented band here in the city of Jacksonville). And as I was getting ready to cross the Buckman Bridge, my phone rang and I was excited to hear whatever it was my mom was going to talk about. So as the conversation went on, she was free with her words going down memory lane, and I'm just listening and hanging on to every word. I think we were talking about food and the subject of weight came up, and she began to talk about the night I was born.

She said, "You know, Gay-Gay (yes that's my family nickname), I remember I was in a lot of pain!" It's funny because growing up, she would always say, "I love hanging out in the streets with my friends because I was born in the ambulance." However, she went on to say, she woke up in a lot of pain. She got up to do something and fell behind the bed. And as she was falling, she grabbed her stomach saying, "My baby, my baby." As she lay there crying, because she was home alone at the time, she heard a voice say, "Don't be afraid, Kari's full of grace!"

Pause! Okay, now at that moment, I thought to myself why the angel would call her Kari; her name is Sadie! So, was the angel saying, "Kari's full of grace"? *My mom speaks with an accent, so you never know!* Then, I recalled her saying when I was younger that she was going to name me Kari, but my godmother wanted to name me, so she decided to go with August as opposed to Kari. So, now you know the reason I go by Kari.

Nonetheless, she went on to say that the next thing she knew, she woke up in the bed. And when my cousin came into the room, she asked her where was the other person that helped her, but my cousin replied that there was no one else in the house. She went on to say that because of her complications, she had an early delivery. I was supposed to arrive in September, but I came in August. According to her, it was a rainy Tuesday morning.

As I sat and listened, or as I drove and listened, I was in awe because my mom never shared this with me before, and I thought how awesome it was to go down memory lane and hear how it all came about. Even though my dad was acting crazy, his family, especially one of his cousins, just overlove me, and yes, his family showered me with love. I can understand that since I was his firstborn.

My mom said I was the cutest baby in the world . . . Just kidding. More like the tiniest little thing weighing in at a whopping five pounds five ounces, so much so that she hid me from everyone else for almost six months until I put on a little weight! (I was the smallest baby and still the smallest child.)

Like I said before, my mom was a dreamer and she would always tell us about the dreams she had! More than likely, if it was pertaining to any of us, they came to pass! One of the funniest times was when we were all sitting around watching television and someone noticed she was in deep thought. Then that someone asked her what was she thinking about, and as she looked into space, she said, "I had a dream," and everyone parted like the Red Sea because no one wanted to know what the dream was about. Later that night, my friends called to see if we were still going out. I told them my momma had a dream and I wasn't going anywhere. No, we didn't know what it was about and we didn't want to know.

So one day, we were sitting on the phone conversing, and my mom said to me, "I had a dream that you got married and you were so happy, you had this big smile on your face, and you came to me and showed me the pictures." But as she was talking, I thought to myself, why would I be showing her pictures of my wedding, why would she not be there? I didn't say anything. I just continue to listen as she went on to say that I had this big smile on my face, how beautiful the pictures were, and how beautiful the wedding was. I don't recall much about my husband, other than the fact that he made me happy! Looking back, I didn't see the signs. As painful as it is to admit, I now get it! I understand why she was shearing so much history, why suddenly; she wanted me to know.

To everyone who's lost a loved one, especially a parent, let me express my sincere condolences. This pain I know is extremely painful, and every day is a day of healing. It doesn't matter if it was five days or fifty years, pain is pain and there is no expiration date because their memory lives on in you/us wondering the "what ifs and the how comes"! And I know I'm right, because sometimes when I'm on social media, I'll see a post saying, "If my mom was here today, she would be 123 XYZ, Happy Birthday in heaven, Mom," or "This year, Jonny would be graduating high school, R.I.H., my love"! Now, tell me you haven't seen it! So, don't say it doesn't matter; it matters! So, to those who haven't experience this great of a loss, please don't dummy down someone else's grieving process! Just continue to pray for their strength in the Lord! They say, "Time heals all wounds," but time is not on my side!

CHAPTER 24

A CALL TO PRAYER

I know God has a call on my life, and I'm not saying that to be deep! I mean, God has a calling on all of us. In this season, I was called as an intercessor to pray on behalf of God's people. There's a mantle that is resting on me. I know because I can pray and believe God for you faster than I do for myself. When God puts people in my spirit, I don't hesitate to pray for them. Sometimes, I'd reach out to them, letting them know they were on my mind, and without fail, they will open in one way or another! I didn't or don't do it to pry, because whatever someone shares with me stays with me! And I truly believe that's why God trusts me with this praying assignment.

Looking back, I can remember it like yesterday. I was around sixteen. I woke up one early morning to use the restroom, and as I was leaving, I opened the door and this bright light about the size of a grapefruit came out of nowhere (the house was dark), as if it fell from the ceiling, and hit me in the face. When I opened my eyes, I was lying on the floor. I don't know how long I was down there, but I woke up with my hands lifted over my head as if someone laid hands on me and I was out in the spirit. I felt nothing; no pain, no backache, nothing! When I realized that I was on the floor, I jumped up and ran to close the door in fear because I didn't know *what* it was! I know it wasn't the light from the ceiling because you had to pull the string to turn it on and it was still in place. As I looked around, there was nothing there.

It wasn't a hit like something you feel; it was more of a feather or a puff of air. I really can't explain it like how I felt it. I stood there shaking, trying to understand what had just happened. I opened the door slowly with a crack to peep through, but I saw nothing! Then, I opened it fully, still slowly looking around to see if it was going to happen again. "Am I going crazy?" is what I kept asking myself, because at this point, I'm starting to think I am! I didn't see anything, so I ran into my room, jumped in the bed, and pulled the covers over my head, still trying to figure out what just happened. I couldn't sleep, so I just lay there. When the day broke, I went and woke my mom out of her sleep! (I'm laughing now, looking back.) I was shaking her as I whispered, "Mummy, Mummy, wake up, a light hit me in my face." She said, "What?" And I tried to explain to her what had happened, but she also looked at me like I was crazy, so I had to walk her through everything that happened. I don't know if she believed me or not, but when she got up, she got her oil, anointed my head, and prayed for me. Later that day, she called her pastor and told her what had happened. I remember her saying that the pastor wanted to see me, but I don't remember if I ever met with her or not.

For years, I had no memory of that night, until one day, I called home and my Aunt Phinea was there. Sadly, I didn't remember who she was! She said, "August, you don't remember me?" I was like, "Nope!" So she said, "Remember that day when the light hit you in the bathroom and you came and told your mummy?" I said, "What light?" And she repeated everything I said to my mother. When she said those words, everything came rushing back! I didn't even remember she was there! Thinking *wow,* that really happened! Throughout the years, I would think about it from time to time, but I really didn't dwell on it until I gave my life to Christ! New in Christ, I really wanted to know what that night was all about, so one day, I went and talked to my pastor about it, and he said, "Maybe that's God's way of letting you know he's really in your life." I'm thinking, "Okay, what else you got?" because I really wanted to know if there was more! Since nothing else came about it at the time, I thought maybe that's all it was! Well, that was it for that season, because that's all I needed to know at that time.

I believe that I went through some of the things I went through because God put something in me a long time ago. I understand now that it wasn't just a calling, but I was called and chosen, and the enemy knew it and has been fighting me every step of the way, but I didn't give up. I was knocked down plenty of times, but I got back up! I felt like the man with the footprints in the sand. When I felt like I couldn't make it, Jesus was carrying me the entire time. Sometimes, I didn't have the strength to fight and there were times I wanted to throw in the towel, but instead, I used it to whip the sweat from my brow and I kept on fighting. How, you ask? As I've said before, going to church and listening to the word, reading my Bible, praying (praying for others), fasting, and staying active in ministry. I devoted my life to Christ, and he kept me in spite of me! *God* is *faithful*!

About two years into salvation, the Lord called me to a three-day fast. Yes, the Lord, because I would never volunteer to go three days without food! At first I thought it was my imagination because I've never done that before. But once I accepted the assignment, God showed me different people's faces in prayer. It was like looking at pictures or watching a movie; that's just how clear they were. And every time I saw a different face, I would pray.

I would periodically fast, but a few years later, he called me to another fast. This time, it was a three-day fast and shut-in (in my home) for the weekend. I would stay locked up in my room praying before the Lord and reading my Bible with no phone calls or TV time, unless it was a Gospel channel. At first I didn't realize it was every month until my roommate Mel at the time mentioned something to me about it. She felt as if I was being distant or didn't want to be bothered, but that was so not the case. It put a strain on our relationship, but I had to explain to her that it wasn't personal. I was just doing what God called me to do even though I didn't know why! However, it went on from the month of March to the end of December.

One Sunday morning during service, I was sitting on the opposite side of the church from where I would normally sit. As I sat there playing with my goddaughter, she was a baby at the time, someone came and told me that First Lady Hall wanted me in the office. I thought it was strange for her to call me out of service during that time, and my mind started running sixty miles per hour trying to figure out why! When I got in the office, she asked me to go in with the mothers and missionary for prayer! My body went into shock because I couldn't believe it. I asked, "You want me to go in the office with intercessors?" And she said, "Yes, the Lord put you in my spirit and I want you to pray with them." I went in shock because I couldn't believe that she would choose me of all people.

At that time, the mothers of the church along with the missionaries would meet in Pastor Hall's office for prayer during the service, and after he finished ministering the word, they would come out and minister at the altar during the altar call. I didn't minister at the altar at that time because I was still learning the ropes. Another reason I considered it to be an honor was when this ministry was first born, there were only a few that were selected to go in. As a matter of fact, one of the sisters shared with me that she wanted to be a part of this ministry, but when she went to First Lady Hall, she denied her request. So, for her to consider me for the task was indeed an honor. Nevertheless, after I came out of my shock, I gave her a hug and said thank you!

From there is where the "altar workers ministry" was birthed, and I was asked to be a part of that ministry. Even until this day, I still serve faithfully!

I was thirty years old when God called me to my first twenty-one-day fast. It was right before my thirty-first birthday. I almost called him crazy because in my mind, there was no way I was going on a twenty-one-day anything. See, back then, I didn't realize God knew my thoughts. I mean, I would hear people say, "God knows what you're thinking," but the only thing I was thinking was he must be crazy if he thought I was going to do that! I called myself, trying to block it out of my mind for a few days. I would rebuke the thought, "cast down that imagination," and it worked for a minute because, again, I just couldn't believe he would want me to do such a thing. It was a bit extreme.

One night, during our March meeting services at Cathedral of Faith COGIC, we were standing for prayer, and as soon as I sat down, it felt like my Bible was dropped in my lap and it opened. My eyes caught a few words on fasting and there was no escaping his voice. There was no doubt left in my mind that this is what God wanted me to do. I said yes! *Mercy!* He didn't kill me as I suspected; he had mercy on me. My fast was as follows: Monday to Friday, I ate only raw fruits and veggies at 3, 6, and 9 pm, and on Saturday and Sunday, just water, and that was for the whole twenty-one days.

Can I tell you the first week of that fast, my team decided to order pizza? Yes, pizza! Apparently, my team made their numbers for the month, so they decided to celebrate with a pizza party. I'm looking at my coworkers sitting next to me in the cubicle with giant pieces of meat lovers from Pizza Hut! And of course, they were saying, "Girl, go get you some pizza." I had to build my fruit salad up to be everything. I said, "You know, I have this fruit salad and it is so good. I have some mango, pineapple, grapes, cantaloupe, kiwi. Y'all know I love fruit." Meanwhile, the aroma of that pizza was slapping all up in my face.

A year or so later, he called me to another twenty-one-day fast. I was feeling a little better because I survived the first one, but still, why Lord? I remember during this fast I had my nephews Jermaine and Trevon for the summer. I had so many temptations during this one that I was starting to think it was a setup. It was Trey's birthday, so of course, we had to celebrate, so I had a little party for him. I even baked a cake, but I didn't get to taste it, but heard it was pretty good.

One of the sisters from church invited the children over for a BBQ, so I'm sitting around all these burnt hot dogs, chicken, BBQ ribs, potato salad, macaroni salad, macaroni and cheese, baked beans, special rice, and the list goes on, and I'm supposed to act like I'm not hungry or tempted. I pretty much tried to stay away from all that food. I waited until three o'clock and quietly ate my apple like it was the best thing since sliced bread! I called myself, taking some home to put in the freezer, but there were too many days in between before my fast ended, so the boys end up eating it. Don't judge me! Lol. (Laugh out loud) In addition to that, I was cooking just about every other day to feed them. Temptation all around me!

I can't tell you how many fast the Lord called me to, but there was this time where I was fasting for "one day" and I was so hungry. When I got home from work, my sister was eating some Captain D's and before I knew it, a breadstick jumped in my mouth and I was eating it like it was the last supper. My sister asked, "Aren't you fasting"? I looked at her like, "Am I?" I forgot all about that fast!

Now, here we are, in our women's ministry JEWEL (Jesus Elect Women of Excellent Living) book club and during this time, were reading Dr. Myles Monroe's book, *Understanding the Purpose and Power of Women*. It is an awesome book, by the way. If you ever get a chance to read it, you won't be disappointed. Nevertheless, his teaching gives you a thirst for more, and I was thirsty, so I decided to look up some of his messages via YouTube! Ask me why again later. *Lord, have mercy*! I came across several messages that sparked my interest. One was a message on "the power of prayer and fasting," so of course, I decided to take a listen. The message was so powerful, I was blown away and scared at the same time. That message played in my head for weeks, and I felt it coming, but I didn't want to acknowledge it. "Oh Lord, not again," was my first thought! Sometimes, it's a setup, I'm just saying!

Now, I've been on a twenty-one-day fast before, but I've never been on an absolute twenty-one-day fast. Yeah, I really had to pray about that one. Now, at this time in my life, I was dealing with a lot of hardship, with the mortgage being three months behind, fighting sickness in my body, burying my dad not too long ago, and now my mom has cancer glioblastoma (GBM) cancer and is scheduled for another brain surgery. It seemed like heaven is closed and God was not talking to me, and the list goes on, and I hear, "You need to fast." *Howbeit this kind goeth not out but by prayer and fasting (Matt. 17:21, KJVA)*. I pondered on that for a minute. Then I thought, there are a lot of unanswered prayers and questions, I wonder if this is the route I should take to get them.

Now, I'm praying for wisdom, knowledge, and understanding, but I could feel the pull, but still, I waited because I had to get my mind right! At this point, it's now or never for me, so I committed to the dates in advance. I knew I was going to visit my mother in Miami, so I decided I would start once I return. As I promised myself I would get started upon returning, so here I am now, committed to this fast, and by the end of that first week, I was in the spiritual realm fighting. I had angels on my left and right. I then realized this is where God is calling me. Funny thing is, in all my fights, they never stepped in. They just stood by and watch as if to say, "We're here to support you!"

By the end of the twenty-one days, I saw angels everywhere; they were ascending and descending from the heavens. I was blown away by what the Lord allowed me to see, yet I wasn't getting the answers I was looking for. God was still quiet, so I went on to thirty days. I felt I've come too far to turn back now. After the thirty days, angels were ministering to me, but God was not revealing anything to me, so I had to keep going. I have unanswered questions and prayers that needed answers, so I told myself that the blessing will outweigh the sacrifice. Forty days was as far as I could go, so I pushed on just to see what the end would be. God knows I'm desperate. Throughout the fast, I would see my mother in my dreams, and there was always this lady with a young boy around her. I felt something about her, but my mom was trying to convince me that she was okay, but there was something about her that caused my antenna to go up!

ALL OF US ARE UNIQUELY DIFFERENT!

A lot of us listened to the voice of God as he spoke to Elijah on the mountain in a still soft voice (*1 Kings 19:12*), but just because that's how God spoke to him doesn't mean that's how he's going to speak to you! God doesn't move the same way every time. Sometimes it's in a voice, a connection in your spirit, through a word of prophecy, a vision, or something you could be watching on television! You must learn how to identify the voice and movement of God! You should get to know him for yourself! How does God deal with you on an individual level?

It's just like having children. You cannot treat all your kids the same even though there are parents who make error in doing so. Meaning, as a parent, you have to have a corporate as well as an individual relationship with your children (if you have more than one). Sometimes they might like the same things, and sometimes not.

When I stopped eating fish because my mom made me clean them, she knew the only way I would eat it is if she fried it. So, when she would cook stewed fish with onions, bell peppers, and tomato paste, she made sure to put a piece of fish to the side just for me. And that's how God is with us.

Even though he treats us the same, he still treats us differently as individuals because we all have different needs. What works for me might not work for you, and vice versa! That's why it's important for us to know God's voice for ourselves.

In addition to hearing the voice of God, a lot of people fast, and in my opinion, there should always be a "why" to your fasting! My question to you is, why are you fasting? Is it because of your organization, your church's corporate fast, or is it personal?

Our church organization's scheduled fast is Tuesday and Friday. There are times the bishop would call for a "corporate fast," where the church comes together to seek the Lord! Therefore, we're fasting and praying as a body with one common goal.

Then, there's the "personal fast"! When it comes to this particular fast, the question is, *"why,"* what is your purpose? If you're fasting without a purpose, you're just missing a meal, and there's no spiritual power behind it!

The Daniel Fast is one of the most popular fast in the Bible. Based on the story, Daniel did not intend to fast for twenty-one days. His intention was to stay in prayer until he heard from God, and in doing so, it took twenty-one days before the answer reached him. Mind you, the answer was sent on the *"first day,"* but because of principalities, the answer was held up! *Daniel 10:12: Then he continued, "Do not be afraid, Daniel. Since the first day that you set your mind to gain understanding and to humble yourself before your God, your words were heard, and I have come in response to them. 13 But the prince of the Persian kingdom resisted me twenty-one days."*

Daniel's sacrifice required that he heard from God. It might not take twenty-one days for you. It might take one day based on what you're asking God for, or it might take forty days depending on what you're asking God for!

Understanding why Daniel fasted is significant because he needed answers for a specific dream/vision! Your request might not require the same sacrifice. So, instead of a Daniel Fast, how about doing a personal fast? You decide what level of sacrifice you're willing make because, technically speaking, fasting until God speaks is what I would consider a "Daniel Fast" because, again, he didn't set out to be there for twenty-one days. That's just how long it took for the angel to deliver the message. It became more about the sacrifice, not the days!

Daniel 10:13 NIV: But the prince of the Persian kingdom resisted me twenty-one days. Then Michael, one of the chief princes, came to help me, because I was detained there with the king of Persia.

However, a lot of us are afraid to make that kind of sacrifice because we don't know how or when God is going to respond if we turn our plate down to say, I'm going to fast until God answers! So, what if God doesn't answer you until forty days, are you willing to make that sacrifice? Again, Daniel didn't move; he stayed there until the answer was delivered. Think about it! Certain fast requires certain sacrifices, so let's not get caught up in the number of days. Also, your fasting should incorporate prayer and results in an answer from God! Now, if God calls you to fast, that's a different story. Make the sacrifice because he will place in you what you need to make it through! There's a blessing in it for you, trust me!

I have several reasons for fasting, but one of my reasons for fasting is to know, beyond the shadow of a doubt, how and when God is speaking and ministering to me personally, and how he moves with me. Therefore, that requires me spending time with him. Whether it's quieting myself, praying, listening, or reading the word, whatever it takes, it requires practice because sometimes God might speak one way and then he may speak another.

Here are some of the ways he might speak:

It could be through the pastor, a prophet, a best friend, a stranger, through watching a show on television, in a dream, in a vision, a child playing in the park, or just listening to the waves crash in the ocean! We cannot limit God, because he's unlimited.

1 Kings 19:11: Then He said, "Go out, and stand on the mountain before the Lord. And behold, the Lord passed by, and a great and strong wind tore into the mountains and broke the rocks in pieces before the Lord, but the Lord was not in the wind; and after the wind an earthquake, but the Lord was not in the earthquake; 12 and after the earthquake a fire, but the Lord was not in the fire; and after the fire [a]a still small voice." NKJV

We can't limit God to a small voice on a mountain, because God is bigger than that! That's what he did for Elijah! What is God saying to you? God deals with us corporately in the body of Christ. In addition, he individually deals with each of us because he knows what he's placed in us and how to minister to us according to the word he placed in us and according to the assignment he has for us!

Since I'm a child, the father's voice is very important to me, and I need to be able to move with his Spirit. I personally don't want to keep questioning the voice of God. Not knowing at times can be very frustrating! I don't think I'm the only one who hears or feels something and analyses it like, "Was that me, God, or the devil?" or ask, "God, was that you or my imagination?" especially when I'm praying about something and waiting for an answer! I want to know beyond the shadow of a doubt the voice or movement of God in every area of my life, and that is my sincerest prayer. *John 10:27: My sheep hear my voice, and I know them, and they follow me. KJV*

Don't get me wrong, I do hear when God speaks, just not all the time. Like, there are times when God speaks to my spirit, I know it's him, but there are also times when he speaks, I question if it's him.

Understanding the movement of God is very important. Keep in mind that the Bible is one of the ways he speaks; it's the written word of God and this is what he uses to speak to us on a regular base. However, a Rhema word breathes life to the written word, and there's also the prophetic word. It becomes the revelation to what you've been praying or asking God for.

If you're like me, you really have a desire to want the more of God. Besides the fruit of the Spirit, add praying, fasting, and reading God's word to your life. I guarantee it will open a whole new world for you!

CHAPTER 25

SPIRITUAL DETOXING

I was in the process of losing weight. Yeah, yeah, I know. Hey, I picked up a few pounds! Anyway, in doing so, I decided to do a *detox*. Detoxing helps to get rid of toxins in the blood and liver. Nonetheless, it also helps me get a jump start on my weight loss. (Hey, it works for me.) However, as I was in prayer crying out to the Lord, I started thinking about a Spiritual *detox*. A lot of us fast for the purpose of denying our flesh, so that we can hear from or get closer to God, but may I suggest to you a spiritual detox?

Here is what I'm getting at. See, a lot of us pray, but we are not honest in our prayer. We say what we think God wants to hear, yet very few say what's really on their minds. Better yet, the mind is eliminated from prayer because we try to be spiritual, neglecting that we're spirit, soul, and body!

As I was sitting in prayer, I was talking to the Lord about the things that really bothered me. I expressed how the things and people that mattered most to me died. For example, when my marriage died, blah blah blah, I'm single again, blah blah blah. No more beating that dead horse. (Laughing)

When my dad died, I felt the sting. Although it was painful, there was a part of me that was at ease because we saw how cancer was snatching his life away and we watched it for years. Although the relationship I had with him was not like my siblings, I still respect the fact that he was my father, even knowing I would never have that father-daughter relationship that I've wanted as a child. In my mind, he knew me as a daughter, but never loved me as his child. Even though I later learned to respect him as my father, I still felt neglected because I know that bond, like a broken magnet, was never going to be the same!

The ultimate blow was the death of my mother. Even though I know that death is a part of life, I still couldn't believe she was gone. Just the thought of her brings tears to my eyes. She was my life, my chief intercession. No one prayed for me the way she did. As she would say to me, "August, I pray for you every day, I pray for all my children every day." She said, "I ask God every day to watch over and protect y'all." She went on to say, "I sit and read my Bible and I call every name out loud and pray for y'all one by one . . . I love all my children!" So, who's going to pray for me the way she did? No one!

Every time I went home, I would surprise her because I loved the look on her face when she saw me. There was this one time that was so funny to me. I got to Miami really late, so I went to my sister Latoya's house. The next morning, which was a Sunday, she called Latoya for a ride to church. So we decided to take my car, but I hid in the back, behind the passenger seat. When she got in, she asked Latoya if it was a new car. She said, "Yes, you like it?" "Yeah, this is nice." We're now riding along and she still doesn't know that I'm back there, so Latoya asked her, "Mummy, did you speak?" She said, "Yeah, I spoke to Tay." Then she asked, "Is that the only person in the car?" "What, who else is in here?" When she turns around to look, I said, *boo* . . . "August, gal, what you doing here?" All I could do was laugh. Her favorite saying was, "Go play with your daddy." Ha! But her excitement was always the best "happy" to see me!

Understand why I'm saying "*spiritual detoxing,*" because it goes beyond the surface of your prayers and deal with your truth. So many people are afraid to express to God how they really feel, thinking he would get mad, but the fact of the matter is, God already knows how you feel, what you think, and how you're thinking. There's nothing that you could say to him that would catch him off guard. Now, you can say it to me and I'd be like, "What did you just say?" But God is not like a man. He doesn't think like us. Besides, he's omnipotent (Almighty, all-powerful, and invincible), he's the Alpha and Omega, the beginning and the end! He's God all by himself!

God wants transparency, he wants us to be honest with how and what you're feeling. I expressed that I was angry with God, and I felt that if he wanted to, he could have saved my marriage, he could have blessed me to have children. I felt that it was because of him that I was barren, it was because of him that my marriage ended because I expected him to fix it, but he didn't.

When my mom died, God became public enemy number one in my mind. I mean, who else was I going to blame for her death? Look, I didn't want to hear she saw heaven and decided she was ready to go. There was absolutely nothing you could have said to me, no scripture you could have read, no prayer you could have prayed. I was *angry,* period, point blank! My flesh and my spirit were at a tug-of-war! I felt cheated, like, "Why would you take my mom? It's so unfair." I felt like she had a little more life to live, but it was cut short. If there was ever a time for me to walk away from the faith, this was that time.

Be ye angry, and sin not (Eph. 4:26a).

I had a lot of anger built up in me that I didn't know was there. And when I tell you I expressed everything I was feeling, I meant it! I wasn't disrespectful; I was honest with God. I was opening my heart and soul to him. I was as transparent as I could be! See, I put it, as they say, all on the table. As my friend Regina would say, "Straight, no chase!" There was no room for guessing how I felt.

Oftentimes we go into prayer with the same old techniques and don't tell God anything! Bless my family, my church, the president, the people in my job, let me hear from you more! And God is saying, "No, I want to hear from you more! Open your heart up to me. What's really on your mind?" I know the word says, "In all things give thanks," but he can only take so many "thank you, Jesus," like what are you thanking him for? Some of you don't even know because it's a routine. I know I sound angry, but I promise you I'm not! I just want you to reach a place in prayer (if you're not there already) to where you're free and transparent with God. He already knows what you need! He wants to build you up from the inside, but you won't let him in.

See, I was singing songs like "I Surrender All" or "I Give Myself Away," but they were just songs. They had nothing to do with me personally because at the end of the day, I didn't "surrender" all. I was still holding on to my pain while I was singing, dancing, shouting, and yes, praying! Just so you know, being involved in the ministry had nothing to do with how I felt. It didn't matter that I was on the altar workers' ministry, part of the prison ministry, or an intercessor. At that moment in time, I was only human! And it's unfortunate that sometimes we don't allow each other to be just that! Like you, if you cut me, I'll bleed!

Now, don't get me wrong, because I know this doesn't apply to everyone, but to those that it does apply to, I need you to *spiritually detox*! Take baby steps if you need to, but please, let's get rid of the toxins.

Here's what you can do for a start. Get a pen and paper and write down one thing you know you haven't been honest with yourself and God about. I want you to read over it then ask yourself why! Don't pray right away; just think on it first, because I really want you deal with whatever it is. And whatever you do, please don't say, "I don't know why I feel this way," because you do. That's why it's called a spiritual detoxification! You're trying to get rid of all that junk that's attached to the spiritual walls of your intestines! You want to flush it out!

This will not be an overnight deliverance for some of you. You might have to do it every day if need be. But the more you do it, the easier it will become.

Why do I think it's necessary? Well, as my bishop would say, "You'll never get anywhere with God pretending!" God wants to take you to the next phase of your life, but you're too heavy to move. You can't even pick yourself up. Look, only you know what your "*it*" is, so do what you have to do for *you*!

I don't know what your thing is, but I'll give you a diving board and you can go from there!

1. Failed marriage _____ 2. Single parent _____ 3. Sexually abused (child or adult) _____ 4. Teen pregnancy _____ 5. Rape_____
6. Homosexual thought or desires _____ 7. Sexual STD/HIV _____
8. Adopted as a child _____
8. Gave a child up for adoption _____ 9. Dropped out of school _____
10. Committed adultery _____ 11. Lost a love one _____
11. You were cheated on _____ 12. Loved one in prison _____
13. You were abandoned as a child/foster care _____ 14. Hurt in church/ministry _____
15. You can't have children _____ 16. You were bullied _____
17. You put your life of hold to raise your children, but feel some type of way about it_____ 18. You had an abortion(s)/You asked someone to_____
19. Raised in a single parent home where the other parent disowned you_____
20. Sold your body for money and still feel the sting _____

These are just a few things that came to mind. If any of it applies to you, great, pick one and start from there. If none applies, write your own list. My only desire is for you to heal so God can elevate you to the next phase or level in your life. You were not meant to stay in one place forever—that's what houses are for!

After all, it becomes a part of your testimony, and I want you to be able to *testify* to the Glory of *God*!

CHAPTER 26

HEALING

When it comes to your healing, you cannot look at what others are going through to determine how God is going to move on your behalf. Your faith might not be on the same level as others, but you must know that what God has for you is for you! Sometimes, we look at what others are going through, and if we don't see any results in their situation, we assume that God is moving on their behalf, but that's not always the case!

You must focus on what God spoke to you. I would encourage you to keep a journal of your dreams, visions, and prophecies, and read over them from time to time; that's where you'll learn to build your faith!

I would hear people say, "You should be glad you're living with something others died from!" Okay, I get what they're saying, but why should I accept living with something God said he would heal me from? *Isaiah 53:5 KJV: But he was wounded for our transgressions, he was bruised for our iniquities: the chastisement of our peace was upon him; and with his stripes we are healed.* If I'm healed by his stripes, why should I be satisfied with living with the sickness? I'm not! That's not biblical! I understand in waiting on the manifestation that the issue or condition might still be present in my body; however, I don't have to accept it! The word says with his stripes, "I am healed!"

We don't have to accept it because healing is the children's bread!

Living with sickness is like having someone living in your home that doesn't want to abide by your rules or contribute to any of the bills! They're not helping you with any of the chores around the house, but they're eating up all the food and using up the electricity! If so, I believe you'd need to serve them an eviction notice! Why? Because they don't belong in your house, just like sickness doesn't belong in my body!

That's the same mindset you should have when sickness trespasses on your body!

In the name of Jesus, I don't accept you in my body, I decree and declare that you are gone, you're evicted, and you have no residency here! You must let the devil know that sickness can't live in your body rent-free when Jesus already paid the price for your healing! That's absurd!

I don't care what it is! It may be a result of sin or generationally inflicted! By his stripes, you are healed!

Healing is the children's bread! My question is, are you a child? Remember that the body of Christ is the bread of life!

Keep in mind while waiting on the manifestation of your healing, God might ask you to do something to help build your faith.

For example, he told Naaman to dip seven times in the Jordan River! (2 Kings 5:14) Jesus told a man to pick up his bed and walk! (Matt. 9:6) He also asked the man at the pool if he had faith to be healed. (John 5:1–8)

You should know what God is requiring of you! Your faith should produce action! All things are possible if you only believe, but faith without works is dead! You, however, need to be sensitive to the spirit and movement of God to know how he's directing you in this season! It's like the old saying: "Some things are more appreciated when you work for it." Why? Because they understand the value of it!

God can heal you in a drop of a dime if he wants to, and sometimes he does and you won't remember when the sickness came and left! However, there are some things he wants you to participate in, so that you can understand the value of your healing! Therefore, when the enemy comes and tries to attack your mind, you'd remember what God did and stand on his word! God already healed you, so you can't to allow the enemy to trespass on your body again!

When I would see the commercials of children with cancer on television, my heart would break because they are so defenseless and I don't have the strength or wisdom to fight for themselves! I'm reminded of the story in *Mark 2:1–12,* of how the four men took their friend to Jesus! *1And again he entered into Capernaum after some days; and it was noised that he was in the house. 2And straightway many were gathered together, so that there was no room to receive them, no, not so much as about the door: and he preached the word to them. 3And they come to him, bringing one sick of the palsy, which was borne of four. 4And when they could not come near to him for the press, they uncovered the roof where he was: and when they had broken it up, they let down the bed wherein the sick of the palsy lay. 5When Jesus saw their faith, he said to the sick of the palsy, Son, your sins be forgiven you. 6But there was certain of the scribes sitting there, and reasoning in their hearts, 7Why does this man thus speak blasphemies? who can forgive sins but God only? 8And immediately when Jesus perceived in his spirit that they so reasoned within themselves, he said to them, Why reason you these things in your hearts? 9Whether is it easier to say to the sick of the palsy, Your sins be forgiven you; or to say, Arise, and take up your bed, and walk? 10But that you may know that the Son of man has power on earth to forgive sins, (he said to the sick of the palsy,) 11I say to you, Arise, and take up your bed, and go your way into your house. 12And immediately he arose, took up the bed, and went forth before them all; so that they were all amazed, and glorified God, saying, We never saw it on this fashion. MSG*

They couldn't get to Jesus because of the crowd, so they went on top of the roof to let him in! Can you imagine what that looked like? In my mind, I can see Jesus running a revival at Westjax COGIC and then suddenly, the ceiling collapsed and everyone looks up to see what was going on!

I'm questioning how tall this building was and how did they get him up there! Did they use a ladder or did two of the men went up first and pulled him up as the other two pushed him! I really don't know, but it took teamwork and determination to get the job done! But notice that Jesus "saw their faith"!

Like the four men, you can carry these children to Jesus in the spirit by standing in prayer on their behalf! Romans 15:1: Your prayers can go where your physical body can't! So, don't say, I wish there was something I can do because there is something you can do, you can pray! Pray that God to touch the doctors and give them wisdom on how to care for these babies, pray that God would supernaturally heal them!

James 5:16 CSB: Therefore, confess your sins to one another and pray for one another, so that you may be healed. The prayer of a righteous person is very powerful in its effect.

Romans 8:28: and we A know that in all things God works for the good of those who love him, who i have been called according to his purpose.

1 Corinthians 3: 5What then is Apollos? And what is Paul? They are servants through whom you believed, as the Lord has assigned to each his role. 6I planted the seed and Apollos watered it, but God made it grow. 7So neither he who plants nor he who waters is anything, but only God, who makes things grow. 8He who plants and he who waters are one in purpose, and each will be rewarded according to his own labor. 9For we are God's fellow workers; you are God's field, God's building. BSB

God is not just a healer, he's the healer . . . and we're workers together in the Kingdom, Amen!

EXERCISE

I provided a list of illnesses (because Lord knows there are thousands) and diseases out there. If you see something you're dealing with, address it, confess it, and pray over it!

If you see something that you know someone is dealing with, stand in prayer for them! Remember, if you don't see your illness, please check the CDC website!

ADHD _____ Alzheimer's _____ Arthritis _____ Asthma _____ Autism _____ Avian Influenza _____
Bird Flu — see Avian Influenza _____ Birth Defects _____ Blood Clot _____
Blood Disorders _____ Cancer _____ Chronic Pain _____
Chronic Fatigue Syndrome _____ Chronic Obstructive Pulmonary Disease (COPD) _____ Dementia _____ Diabetes _____ Ebola (Ebola Virus Disease) _____ Epilepsy _____ Fetal Alcohol Syndrome _____ Fibroids _____
Flu (Influenza) _____ Genital Herpes (Herpes Simplex Virus) _____ Giardiasis _____ Gonorrhea _____ Gout _____ Heart Disease _____ Hepatitis _____ HIV/AIDS _____ Human Papillomavirus (HPV) _____ Human Parainfluenza Viruses (HPIV) _____ Hypertension — see High Blood Pressure _____ Jealousy _____ Kidney Disease (Chronic Kidney Disease) _____
Lupus (SLE or Systemic Lupus Erythematosus) _____ Lyme Disease (Borrelia Burgdorferi Infection) _____ Lymphatic Filariasis _____ Measles _____ Meningitis _____ Menopause _____
Mental Health and Genetics _____ Methicillin-resistant Staphylococcus Aureus (MRSA) _____ Microcephaly _____ Middle East Respiratory Syndrome (MERS) _____ Overweight and Obesity _____

Parasites – Scabies _____ Salmonella _____ Scabies _____ Sexually Transmitted Diseases _____

Shingles (Varicella Zoster Virus (VZV)) Sickle Cell Disease _____

Stroke _____

Traumatic Brain Injury (TBI) _____ Trichomonas Infection (Trichomoniasis) _____ Tuberculosis (TB) _____ Water-related Diseases _____ Zika Virus _____

CHAPTER 27

A PART OF THE BODY

I would dare to ask if you don't know the Lord Jesus Christ as your personal Savior that you would accept him according to Romans 10:9–10:

9 That if thou shalt confess with thy mouth the Lord Jesus, and shalt believe in thine heart that God hath raised him from the dead, thou shalt be saved.

10 For with the heart man believeth unto righteousness, and with the mouth confession is made unto salvation.

Now, keep in mind that this confession is a mouth and heart agreement! It's not just something you say; you must believe it in your heart and speak it with your mouth!

A Simple Prayer of Salvation:

Father, in Jesus name, I stand before you as a sinner, asking you to come into my life and forgive me of all my sins! You said if I would confess that Jesus died for my sins and rose from the dead that I would be saved. Therefore, I stand in confession that Jesus died for my sins and I asked him to come into my life and live as my Lord and Savior, in Jesus's name. Amen.

Now that you are saved, the next step is to find a local church that you can connect with. Why, you ask? Well, although every church that names the name of Jesus appears to be the same, not every church is for you! Now, that's not a bad thing, and the reason I'm saying this is because you have to find a local church that's going to minister to your needs and the gifts, talent, and ability that God has placed in you so that the word can be cultivated.

Although all churches should focus on these things, some put emphasis in certain area than others. For example, there are some churches whose primary focus is prayer. Every time you turn around, they're having a prayer meeting, a prayer function, intercessory prayer, and shutting prayer. Their mission is to pray for the body of Christ!

There are some churches whose ministry focus on deliverance and spiritual warfare. Their focus is to minister to people that are dealing with a spiritual stronghold and demonic attacks. They bombard heaven in a different way, but still use prayer as a vehicle to heaven.

There are some churches whose ministry focuses on evangelism. Their main focus is to reach the lost at any cost. They're out in the streets, knocking on doors, or however the Lord leads them. They have a strong hospital, convalescent homes, and prison ministry. Their focus on reaching the lost is not just to build the church but to build the body of Christ.

And there are some churches who focus is on the supernatural on prophecy and prophetic movement.

So again, this is why I say you have to find a local church that will be able to cultivate the gift that God has placed in you, so that you can be a blessing to the body of Christ and not just a warm butt on the seat.

With that being said, welcome to the body of Christ, my brothers and sisters. If we don't ever meet here on earth, I pray that we will rejoice together around the throne of God, giving him praise and glory. Be blessed!

I'M NOT FINISHED, BUT I'M DONE

Now that we have come to the end of the road, I want to again thank you for taking this trip down memory lane with me. I'll be honest, writing this book was a little overwhelming, having to go through the archives of my mind and relive some things I've buried for so long. But with God's grace and mercy, he gave me the strength to face it so that he can fix me. I'll say to you, don't go another day broken (if you are). Allow God to fix whatever it is that's buried in the closet of your mind. I pray that you would continue to believe, depend, and trust him for your total deliverance and breakthrough.

There is so much more he wants to do with you and through you, but you must allow him access to your past, pain, disappointments, discouragement, and/or whatever it is that has you in bondage. Because of what I've been through, I regretted my past for a very long time, embarrassed by the decisions I made along the way. The fact that I dropped out of high school (I did get my diploma/GED), I was fearful of what people would say or how they would treat me upon learning of it. But I had to realize that my past is just that, "the past," but my future is so much brighter! Everything I went through, God allowed. Every pitfall, every stumbling block, ever heartache, and every heartbreak was all a part of my testimony. It's made me the woman I am today. So, if someone wants to judge me or try to keep me in my past, that's on them, because that's only where I've been, not where I'm going, and my latter will be greater than my past!

It took me a little over three years to finish this book. At first I thought of letting it go, so I put it down. Then, when I thought I was finished, God said, not so. Every time I said, "*the end,*" he said, add this or add that! Then, I begin to understand that it was not about me putting it off; it was about different events that were going to take place and, in time, it needed to be added.

SN: Don't let anyone push you into doing something that they think you should have already been done. If you committed it to God, he's working out the details. Just move with him and allow him to bring you to that place in his timing. He's working behind the scenes to bring you to an expected end!

In conclusion, please know that I've tried to be as transparent as I could in writing this book because I wanted to share my true heart with you, and I pray that I did just that.

See, I knew since I was a child that God had his hand on my life, but I ran like a track star, in fear of what that would be. But here I am, testifying to the glory of *God*!

To God be all the glory for the things he has done and is doing in my and your life!

A SPECIAL THANK YOU!

I would like to give a special shout-out to some very special people in my life. I'm going to keep it short and sweet as possible . . . Okay, here it goes:

To my brothers and sisters
Leon, Joel, Terecita, Desiree, Jacqueline, LaTasha, Yolaine, and Nicole.

(Anthony, Diane, and Joel, R.I.P.)

People say you can't pick your family, but if I had to, I'd pick you all over again. I truly thank God for allowing y'all to be a part of my life. We will always be connected no matter what! The blood will never lose its power. #MercedesChildrenForLife

To my nieces, nephews, and cousins

There are literally too many of you to name, but one thing is certain and that is I truly thank God for all of you! The love I have for y'all is ever-growing and unconditional. Thank you for being a part of my life.

Lisa and Georgetta "Jetta"

I could never forget y'all. Growing up in Miami, y'all were my rock. There was never a dull moment when we were together. We really embraced and enjoyed life to the fullest. But that's another book! We took different paths in life, but that's okay, because we never lost touch. We're just a phone call away! I love you, ladies, to life. #ThereTimesDope

Anna, Helena, Janice, Susan, and Crystal

I have been friends with you, ladies, for a long time. We've had some highs and lows, but we always found the road that led us back to each other, and that's what friendship is all about! We can be on the phone for hours and it's never a dull moment. (Lawd, y'all can talk.) I love you all so much . . . One of the most important ingredients in friendship is love, and love covers a multitude of faults, period! To God be all the glory for the things he is doing and will continue to do in your lives! Love you to life!

Kim G.

Oh my, what can I say to my sister, my prayer partner, the undercover comedian/ rapper? The one that gives it to me straight, no chase! Kim, you are a true jewel that shines bright like no other, and I thank God for allowing our paths to cross. You've been a friend from day one, and time and location didn't change that! A phone call or road trip is all we need to get connected!

Beth V.

My number one from day one! You are my sister from another father (God, that is), and this bond is thicker than chunky peanut butter. You spoke your truth regardless if I wanted to hear it or not, and you didn't agree with me just because we're friends. If I was out of line, you called it! And if someone came for me, you let them know exactly where to go (as if I could defend myself, but okay). If we had a disagreement or falling out, a tray of crabs would fix it before the end of the night. I truly thank God for you and for this friendship!

God has placed some wonderful people in my path to help me along this journey, and I am beyond grateful! There are so many others I could name, but it would be never-ending. But to everyone who has played a part in my life, who prayed for me and with me, like Pastor Watts and Diane G. just to name a few, thank you from the center of my heart! I really appreciate and love you with the love of God!

To my church family, y'all rock! I love y'all to the moon! #WestjaxCOGIC

Again, I say *thank you, thank you, thank you*!

And they overcame him by the blood of the Lamb, and by the words of their testimony! (Rev. 12:11a) NKJV

BOOKS OF THE BIBLE

There are sixty-six books in the Bible, and some of you might never pick it up to read it. (I pray that changes.) However, I want to share some scriptures with you from each book. This is not for you to read all at once, but rather simple nuggets to whet your Spiritual appetite. (*Oh, taste and see that the Lord is good.*) I pray that it will give you hunger and thirst for God's word even more, and that it will cause you to search the scriptures even further than you may know God's word for yourself.

Genesis

46:1 Then Joseph could not refrain himself before all them that stood by him; and he cried, Cause every man to go out from me. And there stood no man with him, while Joseph made himself known unto his brethren.
2 And he wept aloud: and the Egyptians and the house of Pharaoh heard.
3 And Joseph said unto his brethren, I am Joseph; doth my father yet live? And his brethren could not answer him; for they were troubled at his presence. ASV

Exodus

3:2 And the angel of the Lord appeared unto him in a flame of fire out of the midst of a bush: and he looked, and, behold, the bush burned with fire, and the bush was not consumed.
3 And Moses said, I will now turn aside, and see this great sight, why the bush is not burnt. NLT

Leviticus

26:3 If ye walk in my statutes, and keep my commandments, and do them;
4 Then I will give you rain in due season, and the land shall yield her increase, and the trees of the field shall yield their fruit. KJV

Numbers

14:23 Surely they shall not see the land which I swear unto their fathers, neither shall any of them that provoked me see it:
24 But my servant Caleb, because he had another spirit with him, and hath followed me fully, him will I bring into the land whereinto he went; and his seed shall possess it. KJV

Deuteronomy

28:1 And it shall come to pass, if thou shalt hearken diligently unto the voice of the Lord thy God, to observe and to do all his commandments which I command thee this day, that the Lord thy God will set thee on high above all nations of the earth:
2 And all these blessings shall come on thee, and overtake thee, if thou shalt hearken unto the voice of the Lord thy God.
3 Blessed shalt thou be in the city, and blessed shalt thou be in the field. KJV

Joshua

8 This book of the law shall not depart out of thy mouth; but thou shalt meditate therein day and night, that thou mayest observe to do according to all that is written therein: for then thou shalt make thy way prosperous, and then thou shalt have good success.
9 Have not I commanded thee? Be strong and of a good courage; be not afraid, neither be thou dismayed: for the Lord thy God is with thee whithersoever thou goest. KJV

Judges

1 Now after the death of Joshua it came to pass, that the children of Israel asked the Lord, saying, Who shall go up for us against the Canaanites first, to fight against them?

2 And the Lord said, Judah shall go up: behold, I have delivered the land into his hand. KJV

Ruth

1:16 And Ruth said, Entreat me not to leave thee, or to return from following after thee: for whither thou goest, I will go; and where thou lodgest, I will lodge: thy people shall be my people, and thy God my God:
17 Where thou diest, will I die, and there will I be buried: the Lord do so to me, and more also, if ought but death part thee and me. NIV

I Samuel

1:15 And Hannah answered and said, No, my lord, I am a woman of a sorrowful spirit: I have drunk neither wine nor strong drink, but have poured out my soul before the Lord.
16 Count not thine handmaid for a daughter of Belial: for out of the abundance of my complaint and grief have I spoken hitherto.
17 Then Eli answered and said, Go in peace: and the God of Israel grant thee thy petition that thou hast asked of him. KJV

II Samuel

11:3 And the king said, Is there not yet any of the house of Saul, that I may shew the kindness of God unto him? And Ziba said unto the king, Jonathan hath yet a son, which is lame on his feet.
4 And the king said unto him, Where is he? And Ziba said unto the king, Behold, he is in the house of Machir, the son of Ammiel, in Lo–debar.

I Kings

9:1 And it came to pass, when Solomon had finished the building of the house of the Lord, and the king's house, and all Solomon's desire which he was pleased to do,
2 That the Lord appeared to Solomon the second time, as he had appeared unto him at Gibeon.

3 And the Lord said unto him, I have heard thy prayer and thy supplication, that thou hast made before me: I have hallowed this house, which thou hast built, to put my name there forever; and mine eyes and mine heart shall be there perpetually. KJV

II Kings

20:2 Then he turned his face to the wall, and prayed unto the Lord, saying,
3 I beseech thee, O Lord, remember now how I have walked before thee in truth and with a perfect heart, and have done that which is good in thy sight. And Hezekiah wept sore. KJV

I Chronicles

22:9 Behold, a son shall be born to thee, who shall be a man of rest; and I will give him rest from all his enemies round about: for his name shall be Solomon, and I will give peace and quietness unto Israel in his days.
10 He shall build a house for my name; and he shall be my son, and I will be his father; and I will establish the throne of his kingdom over Israel forever.
11 Now, my son, the Lord be with thee; and prosper thou, and build the house of the Lord thy God, as he hath said of thee. KJV

II Chronicles

7:14 If my people, which are called by my name, shall humble themselves, and pray, and seek my face, and turn from their wicked ways; then will I hear from heaven, and will forgive their sin, and will heal their land. KJV

Ezra

8:21 Then I proclaimed a fast there, at the river of Ahava, that we might afflict ourselves before our God, to seek of him a right way for us, and for our little ones, and for all our substance.
22 For I was ashamed to require of the king a band of soldiers and horsemen to help us against the enemy in the way: because we had spoken unto the king, saying, The hand of our God is upon all them for good that seek him; but his power and his wrath is against all them that forsake him.
23 So we fasted and besought our God for this: and he was entreated of us. KJV

Nehemiah

6:2 That Sanballat and Geshem sent unto me, saying, Come, let us meet together in some one of the villages in the plain of Ono. But they thought to do me mischief. 3 And I sent messengers unto them, saying, I am doing a great work, so that I cannot come down: why should the work cease, whilst I leave it, and come down to you? KJV

Esther

4:13 Then Mordecai commanded to answer Esther, Think not with thyself that thou shalt escape in the king's house, more than all the Jews.
14 For if thou altogether holdest thy peace at this time, then shall there enlargement and deliverance arise to the Jews from another place; but thou and thy father's house shall be destroyed: and who knoweth whether thou art come to the kingdom for such a time as this? KJV

Job

33:14 For God speaketh once, yea twice, yet man perceiveth it not.
15 In a dream, in a vision of the night, when deep sleep falleth upon men, in slumberings upon the bed;
16 Then he openeth the ears of men, and sealeth their instruction,
17 That he may withdraw man from his purpose, and hide pride from man.
18 He keepeth back his soul from the pit, and his life from perishing by the sword. KJV

Psalms

91:1 He that dwelleth in the secret place of the most High shall abide under the shadow of the Almighty.
2 I will say of the Lord, He is my refuge and my fortress: my God; in him will I trust. KJV

Proverbs

18:21 Death and life are in the power of the tongue: and they that love it shall eat the fruit thereof. KJV

Ecclesiastes

3:1 To everything there is a season, and a time to every purpose under the heaven. KJV

Song of Solomon

1:1 The song of songs, which is Solomon's.
2 Let him kiss me with the kisses of his mouth: for thy love is better than wine. KJV

Isaiah

55:8 For my thoughts are not your thoughts, neither are your ways my ways, saith the Lord.
9 For as the heavens are higher than the earth, so are my ways higher than your ways, and my thoughts than your thoughts.
10 For as the rain cometh down, and the snow from heaven, and returneth not thither, but watereth the earth, and maketh it bring forth and bud, that it may give seed to the sower, and bread to the eater: NIV

Jeremiah

29:11 For I know the thoughts that I think toward you, saith the Lord, thoughts of peace, and not of evil, to give you an expected end.
12 Then shall ye call upon me, and ye shall go and pray unto me, and I will hearken unto you.
13 And ye shall seek me, and find me, when ye shall search for me with all your heart. KJV

Lamentations

3:19 Remembering mine affliction and my misery, the wormwood and the gall.

20 My soul hath them still in remembrance, and is humbled in me.

21 This I recall to my mind, therefore have I hope.

22 It is of the Lord's mercies that we are not consumed, because his compassions fail not.

23 They are new every morning: great is thy faithfulness.

24 The Lord is my portion, saith my soul; therefore will I hope in him. KJV

Ezekiel

11:19 And I will give them one heart, and I will put a new spirit within you; and I will take the stony heart out of their flesh, and will give them an heart of flesh:

20 That they may walk in my statutes, and keep mine ordinances, and do them: and they shall be my people, and I will be their God. KJV

Daniel

10:11 And he said unto me, O Daniel, a man greatly beloved, understand the words that I speak unto thee, and stand upright: for unto thee am I now sent. And when he had spoken this word unto me, I stood trembling.

12 Then said he unto me, Fear not, Daniel: for from the first day that thou didst set thine heart to understand, and to chasten thyself before thy God, thy words were heard, and I am come for thy words. KJV

Hosea

13:14 I will ransom them from the power of the grave; I will redeem them from death: O death, I will be thy plagues; O grave, I will be thy destruction: repentance shall be hid from mine eyes. KJV

Joel

1:4 That which the palmerworm hath left hath the locust eaten; and that which the locust hath left hath the cankerworm eaten; and that which the cankerworm hath left hath the caterpillar eaten. KJV

Amos

9:13 Yes indeed, it won't be long now. "*God's* Decree." Things are going to happen so fast your head will swim, one thing fast on the heels of the other. You won't be able to keep up. Everything will be happening at once—and everywhere you look, blessings! Blessings like wine pouring off the mountains and hills. KJV

Obadiah

1:3 The pride of thine heart hath deceived thee, thou that dwellest in the clefts of the rock, whose habitation is high; that saith in his heart, Who shall bring me down to the ground?
4 Though thou exalt thyself as the eagle, and though thou set thy nest among the stars, thence will I bring thee down, saith the Lord. KJV

Jonah

2:7 When my soul fainted within me I remembered the Lord: and my prayer came in unto thee, into thine holy temple. KJV

Micah

6:8 He hath shewed thee, O man, what is good; and what doth the Lord require of thee, but to do justly, and to love mercy, and to walk humbly with thy God?
9 The Lord's voice crieth unto the city, and the man of wisdom shall see thy name: hear ye the rod, and who hath appointed it. KJV

Nahum

1:2 God is jealous, and the Lord revengeth; the Lord revengeth, and is furious; the Lord will take vengeance on his adversaries, and he reserveth wrath for his enemies.

3 The Lord is slow to anger, and great in power, and will not at all acquit the wicked: the Lord hath his way in the whirlwind and in the storm, and the clouds are the dust of his feet. KJV

Habakkuk

2:1 I will stand upon my watch, and set me upon the tower, and will watch to see what he will say unto me, and what I shall answer when I am reproved.

2 And the Lord answered me, and said, Write the vision, and make it plain upon tables, that he may run that readeth it. KJV

Zephaniah

2:3 Seek ye the Lord, all ye meek of the earth, which have wrought his judgment; seek righteousness, seek meekness: it may be ye shall be hid in the day of the Lord's anger. KJV

Haggai

1:6 Ye have sown much, and bring in little; ye eat, but ye have not enough; ye drink, but ye are not filled with drink; ye clothe you, but there is none warm; and he that earneth wages earneth wages to put it into a bag with holes.

7 Thus saith the Lord of hosts; Consider your ways.

8 Go up to the mountain, and bring wood, and build the house; and I will take pleasure in it, and I will be glorified, saith the Lord. KJV

Zechariah

10:1 Ask ye of the Lord rain in the time of the latter rain; so the Lord shall make bright clouds, and give them showers of rain, to everyone grass in the field. KJV

Malachi

3:10 Bring ye all the tithes into the storehouse, that there may be meat in mine house, and prove me now herewith, saith the Lord of hosts, if I will not open you the windows of heaven, and pour you out a blessing, that there shall not be room enough to receive it.

11 And I will rebuke the devourer for your sakes, and he shall not destroy the fruits of your ground; neither shall your vine cast her fruit before the time in the field, saith the Lord of hosts. KJV

New Testament

Matthew

5:13 Ye are the salt of the earth: but if the salt have lost his savor, wherewith shall it be salted? it is thenceforth good for nothing, but to be cast out, and to be trodden under foot of men.

14 Ye are the light of the world. A city that is set on a hill cannot be hid.

15 Neither do men light a candle, and put it under a bushel, but on a candlestick; and it giveth light unto all that are in the house.

16 Let your light so shine before men, that they may see your good works, and glorify your Father which is in heaven. KJV

Mark

16:15 And he said unto them, Go ye into all the world, and preach the gospel to every creature.

16 He that believeth and is baptized shall be saved; but he that believeth not shall be damned.

17 And these signs shall follow them that believe; In my name shall they cast out devils; they shall speak with new tongues;

18 They shall take up serpents; and if they drink any deadly thing, it shall not hurt them; they shall lay hands on the sick, and they shall recover. KJV

Luke

11:9 And I say unto you, Ask, and it shall be given you; seek, and ye shall find; knock, and it shall be opened unto you.

10 For every one that asketh receiveth; and he that seeketh findeth; and to him that knocketh it shall be opened. KJV

John

10:14 I am the good shepherd, and know my sheep, and am known of mine.
15 As the Father knoweth me, even so know I the Father: and I lay down my life for the sheep.
16 And other sheep I have, which are not of this fold: them also I must bring, and they shall hear my voice; and there shall be one fold, and one shepherd. KJV

Acts

2:16 But this is that which was spoken by the prophet Joel;
17 And it shall come to pass in the last days, saith God, I will pour out of my Spirit upon all flesh: and your sons and your daughters shall prophesy, and your young men shall see visions, and your old men shall dream dreams:
18 And on my servants and on my handmaidens I will pour out in those days of my Spirit; and they shall prophesy KJV

Romans

8But what saith it? The word is nigh thee, even in thy mouth, and in thy heart: that is, the word of faith, which we preach;
9That if thou shalt confess with thy mouth the Lord Jesus, and shalt believe in thine heart that God hath raised him from the dead, thou shalt be saved.
10For with the heart man believeth unto righteousness; and with the mouth confession is made unto salvation. KJV

I Corinthians

11:24 And when he had given thanks, he brake it, and said, Take, eat: this is my body, which is broken for you: this do in remembrance of me.
25 After the same manner also he took the cup, when he had supped, saying, This cup is the new testament in my blood: this do ye, as oft as ye drink it, in remembrance of me.

26 For as often as ye eat this bread, and drink this cup, ye do shew the Lord's death till he come. KJV

II Corinthians

10:3 For though we walk in the flesh, we do not war after the flesh:
4 (For the weapons of our warfare are not carnal, but mighty through God to the pulling down of strong holds;)
5 Casting down imaginations, and every high thing that exalteth itself against the knowledge of God, and bringing into captivity every thought to the obedience of Christ; KJV

Galatians

5:22 But the fruit of the Spirit is love, joy, peace, longsuffering, gentleness, goodness, faith,
23 Meekness, temperance: against such there is no law.
24 And they that are Christ's have crucified the flesh with the affections and lusts. KJV

Ephesians

6:10 Finally, my brethren, be strong in the Lord, and in the power of his might.
11 Put on the whole armor of God, that ye may be able to stand against the wiles of the devil.
12 For we wrestle not against flesh and blood, but against principalities, against powers, against the rulers of the darkness of this world, against spiritual wickedness in high places.
13 Wherefore take unto you the whole armor of God that ye may be able to withstand in the evil day, and having done all, to stand. KJV

Philippians

4:12 I know both how to be abased, and I know how to abound: everywhere and in all things I am instructed both to be full and to be hungry, both to abound and to suffer need.
13 I can do all things through Christ which strengtheneth me. KJV

Colossians

3:14 And above all these things put on charity, which is the bond of perfectness.
15 And let the peace of God rule in your hearts, to which also ye are called in one body; and be ye thankful.
16 Let the word of Christ dwell in you richly in all wisdom; teaching and admonishing one another in psalms and hymns and spiritual songs, singing with grace in your hearts to the Lord. KJV

I Thessalonians

5:16 Rejoice evermore.
17 Pray without ceasing.
18 In everything give thanks: for this is the will of God in Christ Jesus concerning you.
19 Quench not the spirit.
20 Despise not prophesying.
21 Prove all things; hold fast that which is good.
22 Abstain from all appearance of evil.
23 And the very God of peace sanctify you wholly; and I pray God your whole spirit and soul and body be preserved blameless unto the coming of our Lord Jesus Christ. KJV

II Thessalonians

3:1 Finally, brethren, pray for us, that the word of the Lord may have free course, and be glorified, even as it is with you: KJV

I Timothy

2:1 I exhort therefore, that, first of all, supplications, prayers, intercessions, and giving of thanks, be made for all men;
2 For kings, and for all that are in authority; that we may lead a quiet and peaceable life in all godliness and honesty.
3 For this is good and acceptable in the sight of God our Savior; KJV

II Timothy

3:1 This know also, that in the last days perilous times shall come.

2 For men shall be lovers of their own selves, covetous, boasters, proud, blasphemers, disobedient to parents, unthankful, unholy,

3 Without natural affection, trucebreakers, false accusers, incontinent, fierce, despisers of those that are good,

4 Traitors, heady, high-minded, lovers of pleasures more than lovers of God;

5 Having a form of godliness, but denying the power thereof: from such turn away. KJV

Titus

3:3 For we ourselves also were sometimes foolish, disobedient, deceived, serving diverse lusts and pleasures, living in malice and envy, hateful, and hating one another.

4 But after that the kindness and love of God our Savior toward man appeared,

5 Not by works of righteousness which we have done, but according to his mercy he saved us, by the washing of regeneration, and renewing of the Holy Ghost. KJV

Philemon

1:3 Grace to you, and peace, from God our Father and the Lord Jesus Christ.

4 I thank my God, making mention of thee always in my prayers,

5 Hearing of thy love and faith, which thou hast toward the Lord Jesus, and toward all saints; KJV

Hebrews

4:14 Seeing then that we have a great high priest, that is passed into the heavens, Jesus the Son of God, let us hold fast our profession.

15 For we have not an high priest which cannot be touched with the feeling of our infirmities; but was in all points tempted like as we are, yet without sin.

16 Let us therefore come boldly unto the throne of grace, that we may obtain mercy, and find grace to help in time of need. KJV

James

1:5 If any of you lack wisdom, let him ask of God, that giveth to all men liberally, and upbraideth not; and it shall be given him.
6 But let him ask in faith, nothing wavering. For he that wavereth is like a wave of the sea driven with the wind and tossed. KJV

I Peter

5:6 Humble yourselves therefore under the mighty hand of God, that he may exalt you in due time:
7 Casting all your care upon him; for he careth for you.
8 Be sober, be vigilant; because your adversary the devil, as a roaring lion, walketh about, seeking whom he may devour:
9 Whom resist steadfast in the faith, knowing that the same afflictions are accomplished in your brethren that are in the world.
10 But the God of all grace, who hath called us unto his eternal glory by Christ Jesus, after that ye have suffered a while, make you perfect, stablish, strengthen, settle you. KJV

II Peter

1:4 Whereby are given unto us exceeding great and precious promises: that by these ye might be partakers of the divine nature, having escaped the corruption that is in the world through lust.
5 And beside this, giving all diligence, add to your faith virtue; and to virtue knowledge;
6 And to knowledge temperance; and to temperance patience; and to patience godliness;
7 And to godliness brotherly kindness; and to brotherly kindness charity. KJV

I John

3:15 Whosoever hateth his brother is a murderer: and ye know that no murderer hath eternal life abiding in him.16 Hereby perceive we the love of God, because he laid down his life for us: and we ought to lay down our lives for the brethren.
17 But whoso hath this world's good, and seeth his brother have need, and shutteth up his bowels of compassion from him, how dwelleth the love of God in him?

18 My little children, let us not love in word, neither in tongue; but in deed and in truth. KJV

II John

1:9 Whosoever transgresseth, and abideth not in the doctrine of Christ, hath not God. He that abideth in the doctrine of Christ, he hath both the Father and the Son.
10 If there come any unto you, and bring not this doctrine, receive him not into your house, neither bid him God speed: KJV

III John

1:11 Beloved, follow not that which is evil, but that which is good. He that doeth good is of God: but he that doeth evil hath not seen God. KJV

Jude

1:24 Now unto him that is able to keep you from falling, and to present you faultless before the presence of his glory with exceeding joy,
25 To the only wise God our Savior, be glory and majesty, dominion and power, both now and ever. Amen. KJV

Revelation

3:20 Behold, I stand at the door, and knock: if any man hear my voice, and open the door, I will come in to him, and will sup with him, and he with me.
21 To him that overcometh will I grant to sit with me in my throne, even as I also overcame, and am set down with my Father in his throne.
22 He that hath an ear, let him hear what the Spirit saith unto the churches. KJV

THANK YOU!

THANK YOU!

THANK YOU!

CPSIA information can be obtained
at www.ICGtesting.com
Printed in the USA
BVHW031718270819
556933BV00003B/43/P